DOROTHEA DIX AND
DR. FRANCIS T. STRIBLING:
AN INTENSE FRIENDSHIP
LETTERS: 1849-1874

DOROTHEA DIX AND
DR. FRANCIS T. STRIBLING:
AN INTENSE FRIENDSHIP
LETTERS: 1849-1874

Alice Davis Wood

Painting of Dorothea Dix used on cover by Seth Well Cheney (1810-1856)
The Boston Athenaeum (D/5.4Dix d.1845)

Dr. Francis T. Stribling and Moral Medicine published by Alice Davis Wood in 2004.

GallileoGianniny Publishing

To order additional copies of this book, contact:
Xlibris Corporation
1-888-795-4274
www.Xlibris.com
Orders@Xlibris.com
42544

CONTENTS

Image 1
Dorothea Dix from Engraving by R.G. Tietze.
(Courtesy, University of Virginia Library.)

Dix never lost her ability to personally relate to the sufferings of the insane. For example, while in England she had written, "If I am cold, they too are cold; "If I am weary, they are distressed, if I am alone, they are abandoned.

Image 2
Dr. Francis T. Stribling.
(Courtesy of University of Virginia Library.)

When does a man so urgently require the aid of a rational fellow
    being?
To guide his footsteps, as when he wanders thus in mental
    darkness?
Or when does he so much need the knowledge and guidance of
    others,
As when his own mind is a wild chaos
Agitated by passions that he cannot quell,
And haunted by forms of terror
Which the perverted energy of his nature perpetually calling into
    being, but cannot disperse. *ii*

Dr. Francis T. Stribling
1838

LIST OF IMAGES

PREFACE

While researching my book, *Dr. Francis T. Stribling and Moral Medicine* at Western State's archives, I found twenty-five letters written by Dorothea Dix to Stribling between 1849 and 1860. A quick scan of the Dix letters convinced me that deciphering them would require a great deal of time. I thought that I would have to put them aside because I did not find copies of letters from Stribling to Dix. Her letters could no longer be ignored, however, when I discovered that Harvard's Houghton Library had letters Stribling had written to Dix, and two that Stribling's young son Frank wrote Dix during the Civil War while he was a prisoner of war.

Research on Dix introduced me to her many accomplishments. She founded or enlarged thirty-two mental hospitals in fifteen states, the Government Hospital for the Insane in the District of Columbia, and other hospitals in Canada, Britain, Europe, and Japan. Dix also influenced the creation of fifteen schools for the feeble-minded, a school for the blind, numerous training schools for nurses, and she improved almshouses and penitentiaries.[1] Dix also headed the Union Nurses during the Civil War.[2]

Stribling was the first graduate of the University of Virginia's medical school, the second superintendent of Western State Hospital, the author of a substantial revision of a Virginia Law governing the insane, one of the founders of an association that evolved into the American Psychiatric Society and an influential proponent of Moral Medicine in the South.

It was their friendship however, more than their accomplishments, that most interested me. So much so that I believed how they described it was worthy of a separate publication. My intent in creating it was to add to but not compete with the vast amount of material available on Dix, especially Dr. Thomas Brown's biography entitled, *Dorothea Dix: New England Reformer*, and also to give Stribling credit for his many accomplishments.

DOROTHEA DIX– BACKGROUND

On April 4, 1803 in Hampden, Maine, Dorothea Dix became the first child born to Joseph and Mary Bigelow Dix. Later, two brothers would follow. Her grandfather Elijah was a well-known doctor as well as a successful merchant. In 1771 he married Dorothy Lynde from the prominent Lynde family.[3] Afterwards they moved to Boston where Elijah built a three-story mansion on Orange Street.[4] Elijah also bought land in Western Maine and named part of it *Dixmont.*[5]

Dorothea's father Joseph became her grandfather's land agent, managed his farm and his store located close by in Hamden, Maine.[6] Most traumatic for Dorothea was the death of her beloved grandfather Elijah while he was visiting Dixmont.[7] As his business interests were liquidated, legal battles among his family intensified. Eventually, the Hamden farm and several acres of Maine land went to Joseph. At the outbreak of the War of 1812, he moved his family to Bernard, Vermont.[8] There Methodism and Unitarianism were vying for religious prominence, and Joseph became an ardent evangelical Methodist. He sold some of his recently inherited land to establish a book publishing business, consisting mainly of John Wesley's works and other Methodist literature.

An unhappy twelve-year old Dix ran away from home and traveled forty miles to her grandmother's mansion in Boston. Once there, to her dismay, her grandmother returned Dix to her parents. [9] Years later, her grandmother tried to teach a reluctant Dix to be a proper young lady.[10]

Why she ran away from her parents can only be conjectured. Was Dix unsettled by their unpredictable behavior? Did she resent her father's fervor for his new religion? Was she jealous of attention given to her younger brothers? Regardless of the reasons, Dix turned a critical eye on her parents and other close relatives and found them wanting. That judgment never changed.

Running away from home revealed a defiant, independent and resilient young Dix, qualities that later would serve her well. Other clues to her relationships with her family appeared in a story that she published in the early 1820s entitled *The Pass of the Green Mountain*. Therein Dix described a young girl whose parents didn't pay attention to her. Fortunately for her, a widow, who was tender but still firm and affectionate, rescued her.

When Dix was fourteen, her grandmother sent her to live with her Duncan and Fiske relatives in Worcester, Massachusetts who accepted her without reservation.[11] A confident Dix opened a school there for young people.[12] When she was nineteen years old she returned to the Dix mansion where friction continued between her and her grandmother.[13]

After death claimed her father in April of 1821, her mother moved to Fitzwilliam, New Hampshire to live with Bigelow relatives. Although Dix seemed to have little association with her mother, she did occasionally visit her.[14] Seldom did Dix discuss her childhood but when she did, her remarks often were contradictory. For example, her claim that she lost her father to death when she was seven and her mother when she was twelve.[15]

An extensive network of friends in the Boston Unitarian community was established by Dix in the 1820s. The most important one was William Ellery Channing, the famous pastor of the Federal Street Church, who had an international reputation for his literary and political essays and religious discourse on the Unitarian movement.

Desiring to improve herself, Dix attended public lectures, memorized popular poetry, studied literature, history, botany, astronomy and mineralogy.[16] She became better known in Boston after she wrote *Evening Hours*. Her purpose was to guide children through the New Testament.[17]

A desire to teach caused Dix to ask her grandmother to allow her to use a barn at Dix Hill for a school. She argued, "Why not when it can be done without exposure or expense? Let me rescue some of America's children from vice and guilt, dependence on the Alms House, and finally, from what I fear, will be their eternal misery."[18.] After her grandmother agreed, Dix opened the school and also began teaching part-time at the Female Monitorial School that was very prominent in Boston. Later a free evening school for poor children was opened by Dix, one of the first in the nation.[19]

In the spring of 1823 when Dix was twenty-one years old she was described by an acquaintance. "(She) looked sweetly and was very much admired.[20] . . . "Spoke softly, and precisely, regal stature, 5'7" voice, clear, sweet and low."[21] That same year Dix met Anne Heath, age twenty-six, who lived at Heath Hill in Brookline with her prominent family consisting of her parents, five sisters and two brothers.[22]

Similar to some other young women at that time, Dix and Heath developed an emotional and somewhat adolescent relationship, becoming so smitten with each other that when separated, they frequently wrote each other affectionate letters. In a short time Dix became dependent on Heath to sustain her newly heightened awareness of well-being. Although happier than she had ever been, Dix soon overwhelmed Heath by describing real or imaginary injustices inflicted on her by her family. She described herself as an orphan, even though her mother was still alive.

Attempting to save her rapidly deteriorating relationship with Heath, at different times Dix tried to revive it by including the following comments in her letters.

"You dear Anne, in your admirable mother, have one who may always put you right if you are tempted to go astray, but I wander alone, with none to guide me."[23]

"Oh Anne, if you were my sister in reality, as you are in heart, how happy we might be. I should not then feel so homeless. More than sister's love binds thee to me.[24]

Even the death of one of Heath's sisters did not deter Dix as she remained fixated on her own misery. . . . "think, oh think, of the treasure you have still in possession, Anne. I have neither sister, nor parent, nor . . . . I am a being almost alone in this wide world."[25]

"Do not; pray do not withdraw yourself from me quite now, Anne. The living have their claims and common charity would not allow you to forsake me."

"I have none to cling to, none that I dare love in this world hardly."

"I know not why I am so sad of late. I have daily and hourly cause of gratitude for numberless mercies, yet I feel that there is a void that is most dreary." Writing in her room: "My room is every day becoming dearer to me, and I, every hour, more averse to visiting or company."

Finally exhausted by the never-ending emotional demands placed on her by Dix, Heath replaced her with a new 'best friend.'[26] Still, Heath suggested that Dix "write clearer, be more cheerful and less candid in her correspondence." A greater blow to Dix occurred when Heath stopped using the nickname she had given Dix, "Theadora," and replaced it with "Miss Dix."[27] By the end of 1829, Heath wrote in her diary that she did not even want Dix to visit.[28] A devastated Dix had no choice but to write Heath less frequently. Yet her deep resentment toward Heath did not diminish when later she wrote, "You, dear Annie, do not know or understand me, and this is not strange; for an intercourse so broken reveals but little of the growth and changes of character." Dix wrote that she believed that Heath was "unloving and the most negligent correspondent I have ever rated as a friend." Others did not escape her sarcasm, "I was never understood or known in Boston at any time. I found neither moral nor intellectual companionship." Dix continued, "Many were wiser and better than myself but they were not especially suited to me or I to them."[29]

Desiring that Dix be more social, her grandmother suggested that she "spend three months visiting relatives." Even though she did not enjoy company, balls, or parties, believing that they were a waste of her time, Dix complied, but still did not want to return home as revealed when she wrote, "Home, did I say! The world is my home, I am a wanderer in the land where my fathers dwelt; a pilgrim where their hearth fire blazed; an isolated being, who walks among the crowd, not of it"[30]

Four weeks after her 24th birthday Dix moved into a lodging for young ladies. There she turned to writing. In 1824, she published *Conversation on Common Things*, designed to help parents answer their children's questions. For example, "Why do we call this day Monday? Why do we call this month January? What is tin? Does cinnamon grow on trees?"

In 1827, Dix became severely ill with tuberculosis. While recuperating, she wrote *Ten Short Stories for Children*. Over the next three years, she followed that with *Meditations for Private Hours, the Garland of Flora and the Pearl or Affection's Gift: a Christmas and New Year's Present.*[31]

Although remaining frail, Dix refused to follow her doctor's advice or that of concerned friends. Dr. George Hayward warned "your lungs are not now actually diseased, but your future health depends on present care. The less you do . . . . the better it will be for you"[32] Even her close friend Channing lost patience with Dix and wrote her, "You are of age, and have had experience and have a conscience, and if all these will not keep you right in a plain matter as the care of your health, your friends will do you little good."[33] As usual, Dix did not listen and only slowed down when forced to do so by utter exhaustion.

In 1827 Dix left the cold of Boston for a slightly warmer Philadelphia. Still depressed or perhaps only desiring sympathy, Dix wrote Mary Turner Torrey, the wife of a wealthy merchant and a deacon of the church in Boston, "One by one I have followed to the tomb those most endeared to me."[34] This, however, was an exaggeration because her brothers, grandmother, and other relatives and friends were not in the tomb.

Insight into her religious views was given later by Dix in a letter to Torrey. By now, she had evolved to distrust theocracy, especially those who professed to be Christians. She asked, "Where has religion fled and where is the place of her rest?[35] Then later, "I would be cautious of embracing or rejecting doctrines. Had they been essential to our salvation, they would have been more explicitly declared in the Gospels where we are so well taught of every good word and work." Dix also wrote Channing "A man certainly cannot be religious without morals, but one can have good morals . . . without the essence of religion, viz, real piety." [36]

Later, friends and family convinced her to move back into the Dix mansion to care for her grandmother. Once there Dix opened another school, drawing many of her students from affluent families.[37] She incorporated the monitorial method of teaching where older students helped teach younger ones, thereby giving the older students experience.[38]

Dix's school was popular with parents but not with her students, especially those who believed her to be well-intentioned but dictatorial. One distraught student wrote, "I feel the need of someone to whom I can pour out my feelings. They have been pent up so long." Another, "You may perhaps laugh, when I tell you that I have a disease, not of the body, but of the mind. I am in constant fear of my lessons, I am so afraid I shall miss them. And if I do, I shall lose my place in the school and you shall be displeased with me."[39]

Some of her teaching methods were not approved by adults aware of them. Mary Channing wrote, "Students extremely disliked Dix's 'strict and inflexible' discipline." Even after some students left her school, Dix remained rigid and refused to change her methods, believing in the long run they would help her students. However, conflicts between Dix and some of her students began to have a negative impact on her school. Others remained unhappy with Dix. In 1834 Elizabeth Peabody wrote, "It is amazing that Miss Dix has any success. The students dislike her very much. Dix's righteous ideals have consumed her personality. I particularly detest such a character as Miss Dix. I don't detest Miss Dix herself; however, I think she is rather better than her character . . ."[40]

Continuing complaints and conflicts combined with the responsibility that Dix truly felt for the bodies, minds and souls of her students began to drain her. Another concern was for the safety of her two brothers who had begun sea voyages: Charles on a merchant vessel to Europe and Joseph on one to Asia.[41] Remaining was her feeble but always demanding grandmother. Then her mother died, and although they had not been close, Dix still was saddened by her death.[42]

While Dix no longer considered herself an author, she comforted herself by publishing some of her verses in the *Christian Register*. Still, she did not forsake teaching and in 1835 created a charity school in the coach house of the Dix mansion that she named 'The Hope-well Mansion School.' Her goal was to give moral instruction to poor children and provide teaching experiences for other students who helped Dix organize an evening school for working men and women. Yet the erosion of her primary school continued.[43]

Dix still was not well, and in November of 1835, George Emerson told her, "You are doing too much for others and not enough to take care of yourself . . . ." Channing also remained impatient with Dix and did not mince words when he wrote, "Did you never hear of the comparison of certain invalids to a spinning top, which is kept up by perpetual whirling?" He continued, "It was very natural that you should fall, when exciting motion ceased. When you begin to spin again, I trust, it will be with a gentler movement."[44]

Refusing to take responsibility for her health, Dix transferred it to others, believing that she had spent nearly all of her life frantically struggling with her students, family and friends. Sadly, none of them had understood or loved her enough to fill the "empty" hole deep within her psyche.

Regardless of where the blame lay, January of 1836 found Dix exhausted, dispirited and depressed. By late March she suffered a breakdown, believing that perhaps she was terminally ill. Friends rallied around Dix, especially George Emerson who helped her students find other schools. From that experience Emerson wrote that he had concluded that after teaching for four and one-half years, "Miss Dix was a thorough, successful teacher, and had become rich. But she did not succeed in making her scholars love her."[45] Dix asked her friends to "think of me as an invalid, but not troubled." Some doubted just how ill she was.

Then Dix traveled by boat to England where the Rathbone family came to her rescue. [46] There she finally was understood and wrote that they " . . . affectionately number me as one of their own. Dix felt folded as an infant dear in its parents-arms. Hushed are life's griefs, and stilled, its dreaded alarms."[47]

In letters home, Dix reminded friends how ill she had been and how much she had suffered. In October of 1837, after learning of the death of her grandmother, Dix returned home.[48]

In 1841 when Dix was thirty-nine years old, she volunteered to teach Sunday school to female inmates in the East Cambridge jailhouse. There, for the first time she saw incarcerated insane persons as well as prostitutes, drunks, and criminals, all housed together in unheated, unfurnished and foul-smelling quarters. Dix determined to help even those who could not be cured.[49]

To better understand insanity, Dix turned to doctors who were treating insane patients. Among them were Dr. Luther Vose Bell of McLean Hospital,

Doctors Bell and Butler of The Boston Hospital and Dr. Samuel Woodworth of the Worcester State Hospital. She also sought help from well-known men operating in other fields: Horace Mann, educator, Charles Sumner, abolitionist, and Samuel Gridley Howe, head of the Perkins Institute for the Blind.[50]

Understanding that concrete changes only could be made by state legislators, Dix provided them with examples of suffering persons in specific places. Traveling through the state for three months, she documented the conditions of persons she found "whose lives are the saddest picture of human suffering and degradation." Some "in cages, cellars, stalls, pens; chained, naked, beaten with rods, and lashed into obedience."[51] Many "cold and wallowing in filth." Regardless of what caused their insanity, the insane must be protected from the predatory forces of society."[52] Her documentation was included in a memorial (petition) that she created for the Legislature of Massachusetts. Her efforts caused the Worcester Asylum to accommodate an additional one-hundred fifty patients.[53]

Later her memorial was described as one of the most remarkable documents of the era: part legislature petition; part Unitarian sermon, and part personal justification. It transformed her study of prison and almshouse condition into a fascinating exploration of American society. The polemical religious and autobiographical strands united dramatically in Dix's conclusion that "the plight of the insane compelled her to enter actively into public life."[54]

Believing now that God had chosen her as his instrument to help those who could not help themselves, Dix surrendered her life, talents and fortune to do the work the Lord had called upon her to do.[55] Seeds for her conclusion may have come from Lucius M. Sanger, a supporter who commented, "Woman was last at the cross and first at the tomb . . . ." Or from Thomas Bayley Fox, editor of the Newburyport Herald who wrote ". . . The heart of one woman is worth more than all the heads and hearts in the Capitol."[56]

Only God had filled that empty space in her soul, gave her a reason to exist, and thus provided her with supreme confidence. However, even He had been unable to remove her ingrained bitterness toward her family as shown in a letter to her younger brother Joseph. "I certainly have never from early childhood to this time experienced such acts and dispositions from relations as to create the wish to see them multiplied."[57] Her beloved brother Charles had died five months earlier in Africa after a long ocean voyage.[58]

In Massachusetts and Rhode Island, Dix brought about the enlargement of existing institutions for the insane. In contrast, in New Jersey in 1845, she focused on creating a new and independent state hospital. In that endeavor, Dix was gratified to watch her project begin, develop, and end. She would always refer to the New Jersey Hospital as her "first-born child." Dix frequently visited there when she was physically exhausted and weary in spirit.[59]

By now, no one questioned her moral authority, even when she traveled alone, an action that was unheard of at that time. Dix was always a model of propriety, by nature quiet, soft-spoken, and modest, wearing a simple black or gray dress with only a touch of white at the neck.[60] While she did not excite passions or blame others for the misery she found, she was serious and persistent.[61] Dix probably did not realize that being beautiful was to her advantage. A former student described her. "Next to my mother, I thought Dix to be the most beautiful woman I had ever seen. She was tall and dignified, head set and shaped with an abundance of brown, wavy hair."[62]

Dix did not storm legislative halls, but allowed legislators and others to come to her boarding house in the evening. Some reported on her causes, others disclosed new obstacles; many only wanted information, while some argued their point of view. Among them were philanthropists, political leaders, and public officials who acknowledged her supremacy in such affairs. Some evenings, Dix had, at the same time, 20 gentlemen for three hours of steady conversation.

With those who were recalcitrant, Dix explained, expostulated and entreated on behalf of the helpless insane, as though her life depended on the issue. After patiently listening to Dix for an hour and a half, one member of the legislation told her that he did not want to hear any more because she had conquered him and he was convinced. After such efforts, she needed to be calm and quiet because her perpetual efforts exhausted her.[63]

However, Dix was not immune from making political mistakes as in her effort to improve conditions for the insane in New York. Overcrowded hospitals there resulted in a policy to admit only patients who had become afflicted during the past two years. The incurable insane would remain, for the most part, in almshouses.[64] Dix strongly disagreed with that policy and proposed that a new hospital be built for the insane, but without doctors, a method that was being practiced in Gheel, Belgium.

Her problem was that Dix made her proposal public without first sharing it with doctors of the Superintendents' Association. Many already knew about the experiment in Gheel because they had strongly censured young Dr. John Galt of Eastern State in Virginia for suggesting it earlier. They believed all hospitals for the insane must be controlled by a doctor.[65] Dix was aghast that her friends in the association could believe that her suggestions appeared to them to be an attack on their medical authority.[66]

To calm them, Dix sought approval for her proposal from Dr. Amariah Brigham. He did not agree with her proposal and wrote, "Institutions for the incurable were self-defeating; nobody could absolutely identify 'incurables'; and chances of recovery diminished." Brigham continued that "almshouses were inadequate, but state hospitals for incurables would be just as bad, so provide asylums for all. No patient at Gheel is expected to leave until dead, hope never comes. Do not drive patients to despair by pronouncing them incurable."[67]

Brigham also stated, "She was often mistaken and this has thrown a cloud over all her statements with many." Not wanting to fight with the superintendents, especially those who were her friends, Dix abandoned her suggestion for separate hospitals. In the future Dix, now a celebrated advocate for moral therapy, would work closely with the superintendents to advance their common goals.[68]

By the end of 1845, Dix had traveled nearly 10,000 miles, visiting eighteen state penitentiaries, 300 county jails and more than 500 poorhouses in the U.S. and portions of eastern Canada.[69] But she was politically astute enough not to associate with controversial causes, remaining focused on her own work. Her image could be severely damaged if she alienated the very legislators whose help she later would need, especially those in the South.

Dix commented on her growing fame: She was "well pleased to be beloved in my country."[72] Still she guarded her privacy. Her friends considered her distaste for publicity excessive.[73] Dix wrote of her travels, "I have myself seen more than 9000 idiots, epileptics, and insane in my country, destitute of appropriate care and protection"[70] In May of 1848 she also declared that "my objects and aims now reach the length and breadth of the country."[71]

She was told by her friend John Adams Dix (no relation) "You are public property. The world has a right to know where you were born, how old you are and what you were doing in early life." "The public will claim a right in you, whether you give your consent or not," wrote Mary Turner.[74] Of social events Dix remarked, "I do not like to visit attended by gentlemen who are my friends and I cannot properly refuse attention while in public, nor go unattended."[75] Of herself, Dix wrote, "My wish is to be known only thru my work."[76]

President Fillmore and his wife were close friends who advised Dix to visit them "without ceremony." As she traveled throughout the country, she advised the president of the moods of people where she visited. Other close friends were influential Charles Sumner and Senator William H. Seward.[77]

The most ambitious project undertaken by Dix, and the one that would catapult her onto the national stage, began after she became aware of the immense public land that was controlled by the Federal Government. In April of 1848, according to the General Land Office, it held legal title to 352,000,774 acres in the states. The Western territories, still unorganized

after the Louisiana Purchase, contained another 637,186, 028. The War with
Mexico added more than a half million square miles of southwestern land.
In summary, the Federal domain offered a limitless resource for American
development.[78]

Dix requested that revenues from twelve million two hundred thousand
acres of that land be turned over to the states: 10,000,000 for the insane and
2,225,000 for the blind, deaf and dumb. Her petition to do so was presented
to Congress on June 27, 1848 by her friend John Adams Dix from New York.
He also arranged for 5000 copies to be printed. Her bill would be argued
among the legislators during several sessions of Congress. During that time,
legislators provided a room for her to use as an office.[79] However, Dix did not
enjoy Washington. "Life there," she wrote, "was very tedious and annoying."[80]
Impatient with politics, she also wrote, "Talk in Washington, D.C. was all
about slavery, compromise secession, and the underground railroad."[81]

Not all of her acquaintances cared for Dix. Jane Erwine Yeatman wrote
in October of 1852 that she was "truly sorry I have been thrown with her in
such a way to have to see her as she is, more like the rest of the human family,
actuated more by a desire to distinguish herself than to benefit the suffering
portion of the community whose cause she so aptly pleads. Her ambition is
only equaled by her will by which she accomplishes everything."[82]

Dix never owned a home, perhaps because she was always traveling.
However, she was living in a lodging house in Washington, D.C. run by Mrs.
Johnson in 1849 when she wrote her first letter to Dr. Stribling.[83]

DR. FRANCIS T. STRIBLING

D r. Francis T. Stribling became head of Western State Hospital in 1836.[1] From then until his death in 1874, he cured hundreds of insane Virginians and protected countless others who could not be cured. Some had lived with their families, others wandered about the countryside, and many were in prison. Stribling was successful in those endeavors because of his understanding of human nature and skills as a doctor and administrator. His temperament, passion and determination contributed to his success.

Stribling influenced the establishment of Northwestern Hospital that evolved into The Hospital for the Insane in the new state of West Virginia.[2] He and his directors actively nudged Virginia Legislators to create a hospital for insane blacks. Stribling also produced a plan which was reviewed by those planning Central State Hospital, the first built for blacks in the nation.[3] His influence spread during the 1850's when he supported his friend Dorothea Dix who frequently contacted him for advice as she traveled throughout the South, meeting state legislators and convincing them to build hospitals for the insane in their areas. Dr. Charles Nichols, who was building the Government Hospital for the Insane in Washington, traveled to Staunton to seek his advice.[4]

A contemporary view of Stribling was given in 1967 by Dr. Hobart Hansen, then superintendent of Western State Hospital. "Dr. Francis T. Stribling possessed an uncommon and profound knowledge of human nature, and the importance of human relationships. He believed that the drives, interests, and needs of the insane were the same as those of others and that satisfactions of them through human relationships would help restore their reason."

"Dr. Stribling created a golden age at Western State. He had no tranquilizers, no shock treatment, and knew nothing of psychoanalysis. Yet, out of his simple humanness, he had remarkable success in rehabilitation of the insane. Western State is still not the therapeutic community it was at the time of Stribling's death."[5]

Stribling was born on January 20, 1810, in Augusta County, Virginia, one of the eleven children of Erasmus Stribling and Matilda Kenny Stribling. Erasmus practiced law in Staunton and later served as the town's mayor and as a clerk of the Augusta county courts. His mother Matilda was the only child of Jacob Kinney, [6] one of the area's wealthiest and most influential men. Stribling was known to be a loving son to his father Erasmus, who fell on hard times late in life; an attentive and affectionate husband to his wife Henrietta who was ill for most of their marriage; a loving father to their four children, an avid supporter of his church, and the best friend that one could possibly have.[7]

In 1817, Erasmus Stribling built a resort hotel and named it 'Stribling Springs.' Many visitors from the North, South and Europe sought relaxation and enjoyment of music and dance. A separate building accommodated those interested in gambling. Others believed that drinking the mineral waters and bathing in them would restore their health.[8] Thus, young Francis Stribling was exposed to a world far more cosmopolitan than others existing in the western backwoods of Augusta County. Working in his father's law office presented an opportunity to acquire the social skills and organizational habits that would serve him well.[9]

Stripling enrolled in the 1829-1830 session of the University of Virginia's medical school in Charlottesville, Virginia and became its first graduate.[10] After spending another year at the University of Pennsylvania to obtain a medical degree, Stribling returned to Staunton to practice medicine. On May 17, 1832, Stribling married Henrietta Cuthbert of Norfolk[11] and their marriage produced four children: Ella Matilda, Fannie Cuthbert, Francis, Jr. and Henrietta Bekeley.[12]

He was appointed head of Western State in 1836. Understanding his lack of experience treating the insane, Stribling immediately visited hospitals in the middle and northern states that had some insane patients. On that trip, he established personal relationships with many well-known doctors, among them Samuel Woodward and Luther Bell.[13] Stribling nurtured those friendships and established others.

In late 1836, six months after becoming head of Western State, Stribling challenged his directors by writing them that Virginia should be mortified that it was not curing its insane patients. It must follow the examples set by those managing similar institutions in other states. If not, Virginia's asylums would remain insignificant and obscure by comparison to other similar institutions.[14]

Stribling's treatments included medical and moral means based on philosophy and physiology. "Moral means consisted of everything other than medical ones that could be brought to bear, directly or indirectly, upon the thoughts, feelings, passions, and propensities of the human mind and heart" wrote Stribling.[15] It encompassed early treatment, nutritious food, work, exercise, fewer restraints, access to amusements and religious services and the removal of activities that aroused a patient's anger or passions.[16] Depending on circumstances, he used one or the other, but more often a blend of the two.

Stribling's fellow doctors agreed that patients who worked recovered sooner than those who did not. But providing work for his patients would require that his director purchase more land, construct more buildings, and increase the number of attendants (nurses). They were to be a friend to their patients "because having a friend was so important to a patient's self-esteem" wrote Stribling. All of his requests were granted by his directors.

Just a year later, benefits from Stribling's practices were evident to his directors. In their 1837 report to the legislature, they not only praised him but also began attaching his reports to their own.[17] Stribling took advantage of that opportunity to remind the legislators of Western State's accomplishments and to build personal relationships with them. The more they understood insanity, the more inclined they would be to provide additional funds.

Finding a hospital in chaos, Stribling quickly separated patients according to the severity of their insanity. Created was an opportunity to help patients because of a more cheerful atmosphere throughout the hospital. Coarse, uniform-type clothes worn by the patients suggested to them that they were prisoners and hindered their recovery. Stribling suggested that Virginia law be changed to allow patients to wear clothes similar to those they had worn before entering the hospital.[18] To reduce expenses, he suggested that his directors purchase material so that female patients could make the patient's clothes.[19]

By 1841, the lives of the patients, officers, and employees at Western State had been transformed. Male and female patients were working and enjoying a variety of leisure activities. Soon, they would be eating for the first time in a dining room and attending religious services.

Eastern State Hospital opened its door to patients in 1773, thus becoming the first hospital in the British Colonies to be built exclusively for the insane.[20] When Western State was created in 1828, it was also administered by the Virginia Legislature. Consequently both hospitals would always be joined at the hip with any activity by one affecting the other. From the time it opened, Eastern State admitted patients regardless of their class, color or length of illness. Rather it was based on the date of their application.[21]

When Stribling and young Dr. John Minson Galt at Eastern State Hospital were asked by the Virginia Legislature to review state laws on insanity, Stribling rewrote them. It was important to him to legalize his practice of admitting only curable patients because that practice caused his directors unease. At first Galt and his directors did not object to his changes. However, in short time, he and his directors realized that Stribling was admitting only curable patients and leaving the incurables for them. Consequently, the Legislature would assume Eastern State to be less efficient than Western

State. To reverse that perception, Galt and his supporters lobbied to change the law again.[22] The ensuing battle between the two institutions was bitter, but finally won by Western State.[23]

In 1852 Stribling and his directors were forced to defend themselves from charges made by Captain Randolph that his son had been mistreated while a patient at Western State.[24] The directors conducted an investigation that was incomplete and rushed. Randolph's charges were based on statements from patients he believed to be sane enough to tell the truth. Yet the directors would not permit their testimony.[25] That decision was unfortunate because Stribling and his directors betrayed patients whom they had constantly described as understanding right from wrong.

Because Western State had become nearly self-sufficient years before the Civil War began, Stribling and his employees were able to provide basic needs for their patients during the war years. Their numbers varied between 331 and 376.[26] But the strain of caring for them may have contributed to the physical breakdown that Stribling suffered in 1863. While he did not identify his medical problems, he did tell his directors that it was so protracted and obstinate that for a time he felt unsure whether or not he could continue his work. His directors wrote that "Severe indisposition compelled him to visit Richmond for medical and surgical assistance." Afterward he recovered.[27]

Stribling and his employees were devastated on March 5, 1865, when General Philip Sheridan's troops sacked their hospital, taking food, clothes, animals and farm equipment. Stribling's account of the incident follows. "A detachment from General Sheridan's command made an assault upon the meat house, flour house, storeroom and other out buildings; bearing off and destroying about 180 barrels of flour, 10,600 pounds of bacon, 300 bushels of corn, a considerable quantity of eggs, 135 bushes of rye and oats, 3 valuable mules, wagons and carriage harness, 50 pairs of coarse shoes, and many articles of wearing apparel from the laundry."

Stribling promptly described his institution to the officer in command and told him how many insane patients were there. He also told him how difficult it had been to obtain the supplies; and if removed, he might be unable to replace them. His words were without avail. However, Stribling was gratified that the soldiers did not enter the buildings occupied by patients. The Federal privates had been more patient than the officers, who had shown no restraint.

The act of the Federal soldiers had been brutal vandalism because the supplies were not taken for the use of the soldiers, but were destroyed before the eyes of the hospital's officers. The financial loss was considerable. Flour then cost $7 to $10 a barrel; bacon, 12 1/2 cents a pound; and corn and rye, $1 dollar a bushel even if they could be procured at all. The action on the part of General Sheridan's officers was not excusable under any pleas of military necessity.[28]

The war was nearly over on April 15, 1865, after General Robert E. Lee surrendered to General Ulysses S. Grant at Appomattox.[29] Now however, Stribling entered a time of professional and personal stress. The former Virginia legislature that had supported him for so many years no longer existed so he was forced to deal with the new Pierpont government in Richmond. Because Stribling was a former officer of the Confederacy, he was in grave danger of losing his job. And at a time when his wife's health was worsening and his own deteriorating, he needed more help at home that formerly had been supplied by his personal slaves who were now free.

In 1868, Stribling was honored when the Superintendents' Association invited him to give a speech at their annual meeting on June 23 in Boston.

The *Enquirer and Examiner* newspaper in Boston described Stribling's speech as brief but excellent, and printed it in its entirety. It follows unedited.

> If, gentlemen, any unkind feeling may have been engendered by the sectional strife's of the past, it is delightful to perceive that such have been dismissed from our minds and hearts. The unhappy controversy, which for four heavy years, divided and distracted the country having ceased, it is the duty of all good citizens to endeavor to blot out as far as may be practicable all bitter memories."
>
> This is especially incumbent on an association like ours. Dedicated as our lives have been to one of the noblest of Christian charities, the acerbities of partisan politics can receive no countenance

from the members of this association. Called to minister to minds diseased, it would be strange indeed, if we could so far forget our appropriate office as to stimulate those vile passions which have driven a nation to frenzy. On the contrary, let us bring our united efforts to the task of soothing popular excitement, of pouring oil on the troubled waters, and of inculcating 'peace on earth and good will towards men.'

This is our appropriate mission. Nations, like individuals, are subject to paroxysms of insanity; and nations, like individuals, require a judicious system of moral treatment; and while we may not feel justified in taking charge of the nation and prescribing those remedies which are necessary to restore the national mind to a healthy condition, we can at least so employ the limited means at our command as not to aggravate the malady."

We can give expression to sentiments of charity, and teach the necessity for mutual forbearance. We can in our persons set examples of forgetfulness and forgiveness of injuries, real or imaginary. We can cherish among ourselves feelings of mutual friendship and regard, and when we return to our respective spheres of duty, we can carry back with us pleasant memories of our social intercourse, a more catholic spirit of nationality, and a more earnest purpose so far in us lies to restore fraternal feelings to our lately dismembered country."

Stribling's remarks were received by the association with applause, and its members directed that his speech should be a part of their records, as well as how it had been received by its members.[30]

Stribling also began the process of petitioning Congress to remove his political disability.[31] It is not surprising that he fought to keep his position. It was a lucrative one, especially at that time even though the value of his assets had decreased during the war, as they had for nearly everyone else in the defeated South.

Another example of the high esteem his fellow doctors held for Stribling occurred in 1869 when they held their annual meeting in Staunton.[32]

Even after the Confederacy lost the war, Stribling did not change his mind concerning slavery. And during the 1873 meeting of the superintendents' association, he defended it. "Insanity had greatly increased in the black population of Virginia. But that did not surprise him because the owners of

slaves had supplied them with prompt and skillful medical attention, and
kindly nursed them when they were sick. Presently, blacks were thrown upon
their own resources for food and clothes; and when they were sick, there
was no one to care for them. As a general thing they (blacks) were thriftless,
and those who received good wages for their labor often squandered their
money, taking no thought for the morrow. Poverty, intemperance, exposure,
absence of all comforts, and of the necessaries of life, followed by ill health,
and mental derangement often resulted."[33]

Although Stribling often disparaged blacks as he did above, it was largely
due to his efforts and those of his directors that Central State Hospital for
insane blacks would be built later in Petersburg, Virginia.[34] However, it was
unfortunate that Stribling had not noticed, or noticed and did not comment
that since the war ended, freed blacks in his own community had been
building schools and churches, and some had opened businesses. After the
war, others had been elected to the Virginia State Legislature.

When Stribling became ill in the summer of 1874, his family and friends
hoped that he would soon recover, but he did not encourage them. He died on
July 23.[35] Staunton mourned the death of one of its most prominent citizens.
Merchants closed their businesses while the funeral took place. Stribling's
high regard in the community is shown by the following statements selected
from his memorials.

His patience never grew weary and his love never grew cold. His
perception was almost intuitive, and his judgment was rarely at fault.
Possessing great equanimity of temper, he was always calm, patient and
forbearing; and while he governed with a firm hand, the charm of his manner
divested authority of all semblance of harshness.[36]

We speak of men as great, who are only great in destroying human life
and human happiness. But here was a Christian man, who devoted all the
powers of his body and the faculties of his mind. His success was so great that
other institutions followed his example, and at the time of his death, Western
State was second to no other similar institution in the country.[37]

Naturally genial, his life of heavy responsibility never subdued the
cheerful vein of mirth, which was a prominent trait of his disposition. Nor
did it ever render him irritable or impatient. So uniformly urban and serene

was his temper, that I do not believe he was even known to be angry with anyone, child or servant. He was a kind, generous, sympathizing life-long friend; a gentle, indulgent father; a tender, solicitous loving husband, and a humble, consistent Christian.

Under his hand, everything was so perfect in its working that even today, as city church bells toll for his funeral, that immense asylum with its hundreds of patients and officers and attendants is moving with the regularity of clock-work, while the master hand that set all in motion, is lying cold in death. However, his work was not accomplished without sacrifice and the severe physical and mental strain that it entailed.[38]

Of Stribling's professional character, the celebrated Dr. Kirkbride of Philadelphia lately said that, "Stribing stands at the head of his profession in America."[39]

Henrietta Stribling died in 1889. Her obituary read, "Mrs. Henrietta F. Stribling, relict of the late distinguished Dr. Francis T. Stribling died at her residence, No. 10 Market Street, yesterday morning at 3 o'clock in her 76th year. She was a Miss Cuthbert of Norfolk. A large portion of her life she had been an invalid. She was one of the oldest members of Trinity Church and her Christian character shone in all the relations of life."[40]

THE DIX-STRIBLING FRIENDSHIP

D ix and Stribling may have met at a meeting of The Association of Medical Superintendents of American Institutions for the Insane. Salutations and complimentary closings of their early letters, and an absence of personal confidences, suggest that for a time they were mere acquaintances rather than close friends. At the time their correspondence began in 1849, Dix was forty-seven years old and Stribling thirty-nine. Life experiences of each at that time, especially those of Dix, provide insight as to the nature of their friendship.

Yet it was their common desire to relieve the suffering of the insane that became the foundation on which their friendship rested. It was a friendship so profound that both felt comfortable sharing their unfettered thoughts on a variety of subjects: opinions on national politics, activities of family and friends and even gossip about their peers.

As Dix observed how Stribling treated his patients and administered his hospital, she became convinced that Western State could serve as an example for the new hospitals for the insane in the South. Therefore she continually asked Stribling to share his experiences with the young, inexperienced superintendents who soon would be heading them. Dix also sought his opinions on hospital design and construction, selection of superintendents and procedures they should incorporate into their practices.

Over time, Dix would become more and more dependent on Stribling, writing him twice as many letters as he wrote to her, and sometimes chiding him for not writing more often. Especially revealing is evidence that in spite of her accomplishments over the years and efforts by her friends to help her, Dix tenaciously clung to unpleasant memories of her past as though their absence would be more painful than their existence.

The Dix-Stribling letters are presented unedited with comments only to place them into historical perspective. Two letters written by Stribling's young son Frank to Dix while he was a prisoner of war and one that Mrs. Stribling wrote to her son are included. Her letter is probably representative of thousands written by other mothers to their sons in both the North and South. Comments suggest that many more letters were written but have been destroyed or lost. Indecipherable words are shown by ellipses.

THE LETTERS

Dix: January 29, 1849, Washington, D.C., Dear Sir, I have just visited the jail in Alexandria where I found an insane man whose state awakens sympathy and requires relief. I believe that his case has already been reported to you. I understand from the jailer, who is a decent and humane man, that the sheriff of the county has been informed that there were no vacancies either at Williamsburg or at Staunton. I have written to Dr. Galt for certain information and now address you to urge, if there can be no place for this patient at the Eastern Asylum, you will receive him in the Western (State), at least to give him a trial for benefit or incarceration.

I understand that he was moved from his house about fifteen years since, and his head injured considerably. At the time this occurred, his injuries consequences upon his mind were noticed. Ten years since he was employed as engineer upon a small steam tugboat. The day after taking his newly acquired wife on board, he assumed his duties. On the first trip, the boiler burst, the wife was killed, several persons injured, but he himself escaped. The mental distress under which he then suffered has been wholly now allayed. Several months since, insanity was developed and he was thought to be dangerous and an unsafe neighbor. Accordingly, he was as common under like circumstances, committed to the jail.

The keeper, desirous of doing anything for his relief within his ability, took to him a physician whose prescriptions evidently were beneficial. After a little, improvement ceased to advance, and he was evidently much worse.

It appeared that the mother, whose visits were allowed from humanity, had consulted a fortuneteller. She pronounced the patient not insane, but wicked or 'bewitched.' The mother was, on her side, cautious to administer certain powder which in due time was to effect a cure. This she did for some weeks, undiscovered. But finally, the concern of the jailer for the patient, and close observation led to the discovery. He seized some powder that this careless woman had brought upon her last week, and forbidding her to use the . . . . the deleterious medicine that it was not right (and he) analyzed it in order to know what real harm it had done.

I do not know that the afflicted patient could be restored, but I am confident that should he be under hospital care, could become a useful laborer upon the farm. I beg if (it) is possible for you to receive him (and hope that) you will not decline. There (is) absolutely no vacancy at Williamsburg, where he should perhaps be sent, this being the Eastern district. The jailer at Alexandria, on authority of the sheriff, reports a very distressing case of insecurity in the jail in . . . County. Please let me hear shortly, Very respectfully, DL Dix.

PS—Please present my kind regards and friendly remembrances to Mrs. Stribling and to the Matron at the hospital. If I can get . . . my Bill, I think that it will pass, but now see many obstacles are in the way to its right passage.

The 1850s

As described earlier, in 1852, Captain V.M. Randolph published a pamphlet accusing Stribling and Western State employees of abusing his son and other patients. By including two letters that he wrote Dix, he attempted to involve her in the controversy. Dix was informed of the results of the investigation by Stribling in his letter to her of March 8, 1853.[1]

Stribling admitted that he had allowed his hospital to become so large that he could no longer maintain his policy of admitting only curable patients. So the demise of moral medicine had begun in Virginia as in similar hospitals through the nation.[2]

In the following letter, Stribling seemed to be replying to a letter from Dix that has not surfaced.

Stribling, July 19, 1850, Augusta Springs. Your letter reached me in the country about twelve miles from home, where I have been for a few days on account of the health of my family. I lost not a moment in replying. I had no idea, of course, that the amendment suggested in response to the appropriation for Virginia could, in any manner, prejudice your bill; else it would not have been made. Your wishes will be complied with. The mail which carries this will also contain a letter to Mr. Haymond, urging him not to move the amendment. While your bill will not benefit Virginia, I do not want the amendment to throw an impediment on the other states since it was important to them. "Wishing you success, I am . . . respectfully yours, Francis T. Stribling.

Dix: July 23, 1850

Dear Sir:

I sent you the other day a very hastily written page. An answer to which reached me yesterday. I am confident that you would still accord me your views, as you did this past year when you read and we discussed the bill. I should doubt if it could pass with special amendments for each state.

We must take some things on trust, and often be satisfied to do the things we must. And after, be satisfied to do the best we can under the circumstances. I cannot suppose any state bill against its interest when so much is involved as is the case in respect to all the large states, especially.

I hope for the passage of this bill through the House or Senate this session, but it is doubtful for the Compromise Bill seemed to engage all minds or at least to consume all time.

Your absence from the sanctuary of the Brotherhood (other superintendents) at Boston was, I understand, regretted by all who have known you. It is said that the discussions were as sensitive as the recreations were lively and pleasant."

(Because a great deal of her letter was damaged by water, a summary of some of her legible comments follows.)

'Dix had written to the Doctor at the Virginia School for the Deaf and Blind. She kept up with the progress of some of the young women she had brought there.

Dix expressed her concerns about the qualifications and reputation of the architect constructing the hospital in North Carolina.'

I must bid you farewell with all good wishes. DL Dix.

The second letter in the collection damaged by water follows. Legible sections are presented and others summarized.

Dix: Washington, DC, Sept 21, 1850

My Dear Sir:

I received last evening your letter referring to various topics of much interest.

I am very sad to learn that Mrs. Stribling has suffered ill health, and trust she has found permanent relief from the medical influence which you have adopted.

Should I come to Staunton, which I very much wish? I should have great pleasure if all domestic circumstances make it suitable at the time. Is being your guest at your purpose, always recollecting that I have come informally, quite like a familiar family friend. I have sent things today to you for Hettie. And for your hospital which relate to hospital lectures throughout our country.

In regard to North Carolina, I have great anxiety. I regard nothing too great a sacrifice for assisting a really good and modern institution in the Carolina's.

I have written several letters to Governor and Mr.Mordecci risking their displeasure rather than failing to impose them with the danger to which their work is exposed.

I shall be glad to hear from you though I shall be moving from point to point till the last of November, when I regret to say, I shall probably be compelled to return to Washington. The bill undoubtedly will be deferred. I have seen Mr. Steward who is likely to be very popular in Washington, as through the country.

I can get a letter in Boston about the middle of November. Any letters addressed to Dr. can be forwarded to New York or Connecticut. I have very much anticipated recess. Cordial regards to Mrs. Stribling, I am your friend sincerely, DL Dix.

Dix wrote Stribling several letters in 1852. Subjects included her efforts to travel to Staunton to bring two young women to Virginia's Institution for the Deaf and Blind and her strong opposition to a new policy being considered by the superintendents' association. An extremely personal comment by Dix describes the positive effect that the Stribling family has had on her self-esteem, an unusual admission by the usually private Dix.

Stribling only wrote one to Dix that year, perhaps because he was engaged in defending himself from Randolph's charges. The following letter is one of many where Dix requested Stribling to write more often. She also requested that he send information to the young doctors who would be heading her new hospitals. It also contains an unusual comment about her health that had always been fragile.

Dix: February 7, 1852, Washington, D.C., My dear Sir, it is so long since I have heard from you, that I would be especially grateful in getting word of yourself and your affairs. Also, I shall like two copies of your last report, with my name penciled in the corner and addressed on the wrapper only to Honorable Edward Staly, H.R. I would much like a copy of each of the reports of the Institution for the Deaf and Blind.

Will you send copies of your last two reports to Dr. W. A. Chestham, Nashville, TN, and the physician lately elected to fill the place of superintendent over the new hospital there. He is a young man of most excellent character, but not instructed in the care of the insane. The new hospital in Pennsylvania is doing very well under Curwen, Buttolph is a model and our Dr. Kirkbride ever prospers. My Alabama Bill has passed both houses with an appropriation of $100,000.

My health is very unreliable and I feel . . . a . . . release from cares and solicitudes of hospitals. If my Bill here should fail, of which its fate be sanguine, I must I believe, allow myself a visit. Your friend sincerely, DL Dix.

A tired and angry Dix wrote the following letter protesting a proposed policy by the superintendents that would place male attendants on female wards. It reveals her ability to lobby superintendents and her faith in Stribling to undo the mischief being considered by them.

Dix: April 23, 1852, Washington, D.C., My Dear Sir, Your disturbing letter reached me Tuesday in Annapolis from which place I return much fatigued, and resolved to resume my Land bill work next week. It is possible a preliminary bill will pass; and then all day that "once begun easily finished." I think I should not have heart even to write tonight, if your reference to the very singular question assigned a subject for your presentation at the next gathering of your Superintendents, had but led me, in the first place, to desire to quote the desired expression of my mind. In the first place, employment of male attendants upon female patients is, under all circumstances, absolutely unnecessary: this you already know.

Second, it is a monstrous offence against propriety, and cannot be considered in sufficiently strong terms. That it was introduced at Worcester, MA by Dr. Woodward, and has been still continued by Dr. Charles on some of the most excited and others in association with female success, is a fact concerning which our medical friends, who have been acquainted with it, have united to express a righteous indignation. I intended hence to have taken this matter up, but crowding occupations and urgent claims have prevented it. Dr. Ray is indignant beyond measure and yet from his position has . . . silence. The same fault was introduced by Dr. Charles in the Fort Annapolis Hospital, and perpetuated by Dr. Garland.

I have no doubt that the talk has constituted to you of setting forth this shocking abuse in its true light, from your position. Now be advised that Bell, Ray, Barkdull, Kirkbride and others will nobly sustain you, and you will cure that foul malady before it spreads. The same was introduced by Brigham in Utica in the excited wards. I think, but am not certain; it was advanced by Barkdull. The sooner this matter is taken in hand, according to the measure of its offense, the better. You have it at advantage and can silence, Sir, the . . . that is a gross offense against propriety, and the rights of humanity need not be discussed, since beyond a doubt, if harm to be tolerated by superintendent and trustees, it would expose them to those tender mercies of an exasperated staff.

The poor little deaf mute cannot be sent as a paying patient because her family is without means. I congratulate you upon the propriety which accompanies your professional policies. How I should like coming to see the many patients you have, and how I should like to listen to the notes of that fine organ (given to Western State by W.W. Corcoran) and how I should like to procure you the desired lanterns and slides. As in many other things! (One wonders what Dix meant by her last comment.)

I can but add now that I'm your friend cordially. DL. Dix

Note: Stribling addressed the concerns of Dix in his 1852 speech at the Superintendents' meeting. An abridgement of his comments follows.

Males should not be employed on female wards. His experience over the years with over 500 insane females had never required calling in a male attendant to help control a female patient. Doing so was not only unnecessary, but unwise and unjust. Such a practice would outrage public opinion and violate the modesty that was a virtue most important to the female character. It would tend to aggravate the distress and anxiety of the already heartbroken parents, husbands, and brothers on behalf of a cherished daughter, wife or sister.

Stribling was unaware of a similar policy in other hospitals for the insane in the country. Nor had he ever supposed until recently, that such an idea had previously been conceived. Since he could not imagine a solitary reason for such action, he would content himself with endorsing the views so forcibly and admirably expressed a day or two earlier by their associate, Dr. Ray.

In the following letter, Dix opines on some of the inside workings of the Superintendents' Association.

Dix: May 14, 1852, Annapolis, MD. My Dear Doctor, I suppose you are preparing for the 'reunion' of your fraternizing association of superintendents in New York the next week. I wish I had leisure to join you all there, but I cannot do so, to show every possible kindness to Dr. Nichols who has passed through a series of petty arrogances during his sojourn at Bloomingdale (Hospital) that would have exhausted the patience of that adage, quoted examples of his cardinal virtue, the much suffering 'Patriarch of New York.' He and past governors seem determined to preserve a model of 'incongruous' government at Bloomingdale in spite of common sense and modern science.

If I ever get the time, I mean to do something for your hospital. Till then and always consider me then and now your sincere friend. DL Dix

Dix: June 24, 1852, Washington, DC., My Dear Sir, I wish to know if an interesting deaf mute, a young girl about fifteen years of age, an orphan in charge of a Brother, a clerk in the War Department, can be received in the Virginia Institution? She was for a time at Philadelphia, where she became ill, and her brother then brought her home. Since the start of the disease, the brother became anxious to place her again at school, or perhaps at your institution for climate, etc., before any others. An early answer is desirable. In early August, I may possibly bring her {to Staunton} myself in the case she can be admitted. She is remarkably pleasing. In infancy, she had whopping cough very severely, and it is thought that the fluid levels she had suffered in her head caused her to lose the use of her right hand as her fingers imperfectly developed. I am anxious though {that} an August departure is called for.

Please give me an early answer. In haste, but with friendly regards to you and Mrs. Stribling, I am cordially yours, DL Dix.

Dix: July, 19, 1852, Washington, D.C., My Dear Sir, I had intended to leave here for Staunton on Wednesday, but shall defer it ten days on account of difficulty to bring two pupils. And also, I am not well. I shall, if it is possible, leave here a week from tomorrow. That is on the 28th, but today things are uncertain to predict—. It is not possible for me tell when I may be there. Everything is uncertain. Your friend, DL Dix.

PS—I was going to make an effort for the lighted lanterns but congratulate you for getting one without my intervention.

Dix: August 11, 1852, Washington, D.C., My Dear Sir, I arrived without accident here on Saturday, and wish to get some tidings from you as soon as you find it convenient to write. I trust that Mrs. Stribling is more comfortable. My love and sincere good wishes to her and your daughters. Tell my little friend Frank, I shall soon send him some pretty verses, as I understand that he is fond of little poems. Say to Ella that I have not forgotten the promised stanzas on flowers. Only wait time to secure the copies.

I think with much pleasure of my familiar acquaintances, both yourself and your family. I advise you also that while I have heretofore held you in uniform respectful and kind regard, I find my confidence and esteem advanced by the few days recently spent as a guest in your domestic circle. (An unusual comment by Dix.) This I say fondly and truly and I wish to be remembered as being steadily and continually your friend. Your friend, DL Dix.

While Stribling did not write as often as Dix desired, his letters were usually longer than hers and covered a variety of subjects. In the following letter he wrote that he was pleased that Dix benefited from being with his family. His comments on his children give us our first insight into his family life. He appears to tease Dix when he suggests that she might find a rich man whom she could influence to help Western State.

Stribling: August 16, 1852, Staunton, Va.,

Miss Dix, Your esteemed note of {the} 11th found me on Saturday, quite an invalid and this is the first moment that I have been well enough to attempt to write. Although suffering much pain, I am pleased to inform you that my malady is not of a serious character. My wife and daughters were equally gratified to learn that you had reached Washington safely after your hurried and fatiguing jaunt. We are particularly pleased to hear that our little attentions have impressed you favorably toward our household.

Had we done tenfold more than you allowed us an opportunity to do, and with a purely selfish motive, I should have felt more than rewarded by the declaration with which you have honored me, that your confidence and esteem have been particularly advanced by the few days spent with me.

My wife, after extending many thanks for your kind inquiries after her health, bids me to say that she feels more comfortable than when you left, but is still unable to leave her room. She slept tolerably well last night, and this always adds much to her comfort the succeeding day. She says that she will be in a better condition to do her part towards you, and that your next visit not be one of so much hurry and business, but you must make it one of vacation, something which you must surely begin to need.

Ella talks much and seems to have most pleasant recollections of your visit to Lexington. She and Fanny both ask to be affectionately remembered to you. My little fellow Frank often speaks of Miss Dix and asks when she is coming back. You made quite an impression on him. He says 'he will be much obliged to you for the verses you propose sending him.'

I have not visited the Institution for the Deaf, Dumb and Blind but once since you left, but see Mrs. Coleman almost every day. She has furnished me a note in person and asks which I transcribe. 'Say to Miss Dix that I received her letter and will write her after a little more time has been allowed to form an opinion as to the capacity possessed of the little girls. They seem perfectly contented and happy. Miss Peabody was very willing to learn and submits cheerfully to all the rules of the institution. Miss Brown is more self-willed and much inclined to do as she pleases, but I hope that (with) a little training, she will be more submissive.'

They are in safe hands, you may rely on it, and I submit you will be kept fully apprised of everything determined in regard to them.

We are getting on about as usual at the Lunatic Asylum. Your name is often mentioned by the patients in conversations, and many of them, in their letters, make most flattering mention of your visit. Our matron, Mrs. Tinsley, seemed much upset not having seen you. By the way, I trust you were as favorably impressed with the manner, good sense, energy, and kindness of heart of Mrs. Tinsley, as I am.

On the very day you left, and after I had written to suspend further proceedings in the provisions, I sent by mail an account from Mr. Taylor of New York for two magic lanterns . . . and slides stating that the articles had been sent. They have not yet reached me. I greatly feel that I have committed a blunder in this matter, but must have the philosophy to make the best of it, resolving to try to do better next time. I had fully resolved, if it could have been effected, to charge the agency, and (not) bother you with the trouble of procuring for us suitable lanterns and slides.

I am truly thankful to you for the kind solicitude you manifest for our institution, and your expressed willingness to aid us as far as practicable. You have much to do I know in regard to other institutions, probably than ones to help themselves. Should you somewhere come across some wealthy and benevolent gentlemen, who would esteem it a privilege to give us five or six select libraries to be used on the difficult floors, as with Dr. Kirkbride; or a handsome fountain for the use of our front {lawn} I know you will not hesitate to accept it.

Feeling rather nervous to write more and wishing you to excuse the hurried manner in which this is presented, I am, most truly and perpetually, your friend. FT Stribling.

At least one letter from Dix to Stribling was written in early 1853 wherein she agreed with the disposition of the Captain Randolph episode, because he mentions that incident in the following letter to her. Stribling also writes of a visit by Dr. Nichols who was responsible for building the new Government hospital. The fondness for Dix felt by all members of the Stribling family is also described.

Stribling: March 8, 1853, Staunton, Va., Miss Dix, I have received several kind notes and other mementos from you since I last wrote. It has been my wish to write you somewhat at length, and I have been waiting only for an opportunity. But thus it seems my engagements will not allow me, and hence I must drop you these hurried lines.

I return Mr. Graham's letter which I shared as you requested to Mr. Castleman. Sheffy has not been here since being a member of the Virginia Senate. I fear you will not be able to effect the removal of the poor lunatic to an asylum, but your efforts have, I dare say already resulted in improving his comfort.

I was delighted with Dr. Nichol's visit and regretted much that his stay was so short. He has entered upon his important work with an amount of experience, intelligence, and zeal which must insure success. The plan, which he was so good to exhibit and explain to me, I thought admirable. The Metropolitan (Government) hospital should be a model. There is no reason except a want of liberality, or I might say of justice and humanity on the part of Congress to prevent it. The location must be a superior one and will inevitably afford facilities for constructing the buildings and allowing classifying for the patients, of which the present institution can boast.

I am glad you think that we disposed of Captain Randolph properly. The old gentleman, however, is affixed with that troublesome (to others), melancholia. And we will not be surprised to find in print, before long, a response from him, to our pamphlet. [1] Did you receive the numbers sent you under cover to Mr. Stuart last week?

Frank values your notes very much, although he has probably not answered them. We have placed Fanny at a boarding school, and he has to rely solely on his sister Ella to write for him. She promises to do so, but as often, makes some apology for disappointing him. My wife, I am happy to inform you, continues cheerful and is much impressed with 'Miss Henrietta,' (a new granddaughter) whose developments are becoming daily, more and more interesting, and especially to a 'mother.' Your name is often mentioned at the fireside and I am urged by all, whenever I write to apprise you of their regards. Please say to Dr. Nichols that I have been wishing to write to him for some time, and will do so as soon as I can. Present him with my regards.

What about your Land bill? I have seen no notice of it during this session of Congress. As you write personally hundreds {of letters} and I often find it difficult, sometimes impossible to decipher some of your soliloquies,[2] I am sure you will excuse this. Truly your friend, F.T. Stribling.

PS—When shall we see you in Staunton?

Parts of the following letter were not legible.

Dix: Not dated except for "Friday."

Dear Sir,

I received last evening letters forwarded for which my thanks . . . but I searched within the envelopes vainly for one word from you . . . now the total silence is but hard, and I feel disposed to enter a formal charge against your silence.

From Washington the news was not satisfactory. Dr . . . is clearly breaking his fine physical health by overwork and exposure in the hot sun. The letter from Dr. Lopez was not of special movement. He hoped for the appointment in Alabama and I heard he may succeed if he would do first good to the Institution. Your friend, DL Dix.

Dix: April 11, (date unknown but probably late 1853 or early 1854) W. Land Hotel, New Orleans.

Dear Sir and Friend, I congratulate you and your family that your salary increased, as it should have been long since, and for once has had truth in her train. I am sorely distressed concerning the hospital out of the mountains {Northwestern} and if I could by attendance, influence the legislature to cut short all proceedings; I surely would so, even to have the work wait for years. Tis a work admirable, however, yet one consoling, comforting feature in the whole cause/case.

In Alabama, work goes on very slowly. The sole interest of parties' influence is to get their money, with but with slight consideration as to how it affected the afflicted insane. The commissioners, when they do act, seem to exceed the reading of the law, and had consulted no one, when or how {to} order furniture, etc. Meanwhile, the trustees chose several friends since satisfying their friends of service, do nothing except write letters to superintendents to ask advice which they had not the slightest idea of taking, and most likely, they had already decided on the appointment.

Dr. Leland of Tennessee, a doctor of some good qualities but domineering and very impolitic, as his friends, here tell me, and not very successful as a practitioner. He had a large family of grown and half-grown children who were fond of pleasure and much elated with the idea of being in the great house. It so happens that the trustees are not unanimous in their choice to go back this year. And it depends upon those the governor appoints in their place, after all, whether Dr. Leland will . . . replace as for which I cannot learn that he is at all qualified. Only they say he is an "Alabamian" and wants the place!

In Texas, the work goes very slowly, the building of the wall only ten feet {inside} the balustrade. The Texans had done many things well, timely, and wholly. But their hospital was apparently destined to be a failure, and was suffering through the killing influences of politics. No sooner was the present governor in office than he removed all persons, directly or by contact, connected with the directors or confrontation by all the state institutions. What had been studied with care and preserved with faithfulness was suddenly cut short. New hands and ignorant persons succeeded, who themselves said that they truly knew nothing at all about the plans or buildings. The hospital had been totally sacrificed, but the blind and dumb clusters did well. The newly approved physician was, unfortunately, a politician who had had nothing to look at but furniture.{closing not given}

Note: It is astonishing that Dix offered to leave her own work 'for as long as necessary' to help Stribling assure that a third hospital for the insane be built in Virginia. It was completely unlike her to postpone her own plans that were always very complex and involved many people.

The importance of contact with Stribling while she was traveling is evidenced by informing Stribling where she would be traveling next and giving him the names of persons who would hold his mail to her.

In the following letter, Stribling, more politically astute than Dix, refused her offer to come to Virginia to lobby for the new hospital, at least for a time.

Stribling: February 1, 1854, Staunton, Va., Miss Dix, When I dropped you a hurried note by Dr. Fisher, acknowledging the receipt of your favor of the 13th, I little thought that more than a fortnight would elapse before I should again write you. With a desire amounting almost to a resolution every day to write, my many duties have interposed and enjoined one to await a more convenient season. Finding that this season has not arrived, and probably will not, I have determined to procrastinate no longer.

At the proper time, there can be no doubt that your personal efforts, exerted at Richmond in behalf of another institution for the insane in Virginia, will be extremely valuable. I do not, however, think it would be prudent to propose the matter before the present legislature. My object in suggesting it was to attract public attention to the matter . . . inquiry so as to prepare the public mind, especially the minds of the proper representatives, for the next session of the legislature. At that time, I shall feel most grateful for your aid, and will take care to keep you posted as to enable {you} to know 'when and where' to exert your influence.

I send herewith a letter from my friend, Dr. Ingram of California which will I know commend him and his subject to your favorable notice. His mother has long been an inmate of this asylum and you will probably recollect her as a most positive lady-like patient.

The doctor is a remarkable young man for energy of character, is decidedly talented, a superior physician, a high-toned Virginia gentleman, and with a possession of a noble heart. He is interested in the cause of the insane from pure . . . prompted doubtless by its ravage in his own family. I have sent him a copy of the regulations adopted in 1857 by our association relative to the construction of hospitals, and have responded to his inquiries. Of course, there could be no . . . opinions as to the utter inappropriateness of the present location of the hospital to which he refers, or as to the decided advantages of the new locations which he describes.

No doctor, I suppose anyone, would hesitate to say that the state {and not individuals} forthwith construct a new and most suitable set of buildings, regardless of whether they will have to sacrifice wholly or in part their present establishment. I wish much you would write Dr. Ingram at your earliest convenience. He will, I know, value most highly a letter from you, although he would value a visit more highly still. Direct your letter to Dr. Richard H. Ingram, Marysville, California. Please also return me the letter herewith sent.

As to the new hospital in Virginia, and also the proposed surrender of my present post, I hope to have an opportunity of conferring with you in person; if not before, certainly at the meeting of our association in the spring. You will have seen from my last report, several copies of which I sent you by Dr. Fisher, that I continue the incumbent for the present year at least. {Stribling previously had attempted to resign from his position, but did not do so after receiving appeals from many Virginians to remain.}

I cannot answer your inquiry as to Dr. Galt. The last I heard directly from him was thru a letter urging me to aid him in obtaining a law requiring that, in the event of a third hospital being built in Virginia, the Eastern (State) Hospital should be confined exclusively to male patients and the Western (State) for females. I did hesitate to answer, declining . . . to sanction the scheme. It is a subject about which I have thought very little. You probably have heard, read, and thought more in regard to it. And I would be particularly obliged to you if you would apprise me your views in full as to the policy of State hospitals being restricted to only one sex.

I notice what you say to Dr. Chapman's private accommodations for the insane and I will bear your recommendations in mind. There are in this region of country, however, but few that could afford to pay $1,000 per annum for such an establishment. I can well conceive it may be very useful and doubt not it would succeed.

I trust you had a full interview with Dr. Fisher and learned from him many details in regard to the North Carolina Hospital. I fear the patience of its citizens will become exhausted before it is opened for the reception of patients. I urged the doctor much on his return home to put forth his energies and endeavors by all means to complete one wing and much of the center building, as would enable them to put it into operation . . . . now. He seems to think there is no prospect of obtaining the necessary funds. Are you doing anything this winter with your 'Massachusetts' bill?

When shall we have the pleasure of seeing you again? Before long, I trust. My family is quite well with the exception our youngest daughter who is not seriously indisposed! Frank often speaks of you and inquires after you. Ella was in Washington recently and told us that she had called to see you, but regretted much to learn that you had left the city. She said, however, that you were expected back soon, and that if you returned before she left, she would certainly see you. She probably left Washington for Petersburg on Saturday last. My wife, Fanny and Frank all ask to be presented in the kindest terms.

In haste as usual and truly your friend, Fras. T. Stribling.

Dix: April 2, (year uncertain but probably 1854) Washington: My Dear Sir, Do the rules which govern the directors of the Virginia School for Deaf Mutes allow patients from the District of Columbia? I wish to apply on behalf of a respectable widow, Mrs. Brown of this place, who has an uneducated daughter, mute from birth. The child received early in life said injury of the spine. This has further impaired her usefulness. Although her mother speaks of her health as uniformly good, and her mind clear and active, she is already eighteen years of age and of diminutive stature.

Please let me hear on this subject. I trust I shall see you as you proceed North in May to assemble with your . . . superintendents in New York. Have you seen the 'Ohio' report of this year, Dr. Smith's volume? His reports generally are of more than usual interest. Don't you think so? My health is very far from strong, but I yet hope to do much work. With kind regards to Mrs. Stribling and best wishes for yourself, I am your friend, DL Dix.

PS Please address letters for me to J.C.G. Kennedy, Esq . . . . office, Washington."

As to her land bill, Dix had continued to lobby Congress for its passage. After the Senate and House passed it in 1854, her supporters were elated, and she received a flood of congratulations from all over the nation. However, President Pierce vetoed her bill on grounds of future conflicts with states' rights.[3] After her six-year effort under physical and mental strain, Dix was devastated. Losing after being so close to success caused Dix to become so ill that she was unable to continue her work.[4] It was of little comfort to her that Congress had passed her petition to establish a Government Hospital in Washington.[5]

On September 2, 1854, Dix sailed on the '*Sails of Arctic*' ship to England to recuperate with the Rathbones who had nursed her back to health in 1836.[6] The Arctic sank on its return trip to New York.[7]

When she felt better, Dix visited Ireland and toured Scotland and the Channel Islands where she persuaded the governing body to build a new hospital. Traveling alone she visited hospitals in France, Italy, Greece, Turkey, Austria-Hungary, Germany, Russia and Scandinavia. In 1856, she visited Italy, met with Pope Pius IX and convinced him to help the insane in Rome.[8]

Dix wrote that traveling alone in those countries was no more difficult than traveling in some parts of America. She wrote Dr. Buttolph, "I get into all the hospitals and prisons I have the time to see or strength to explore. I take no refusals, and yet I speak neither Italian, German, Greek nor Slavonic. I have no letters of introduction and know no persons or route.[9] I have been greatly blessed in all my travels," she wrote on August 1, 1856.[10] During her visit, Dix had audiences with several of the world's most powerful men, influencing them to help the poor and ill.

Still, Dix continued to try the patience of some of her friends. For example, after spending time with her in Paris, George B. Emerson wrote, "Your mother and I have come to the conclusion that . . . saints are far less agreeable, at least in this world, than sinners, and that it would be pleasant to be left to the folly of our own ways.[11]

Dix could not escape the turmoil taking place at home. "The slavery question I positively ignore." wrote Dix. {I} read no newspapers as ignorance is the best discretion." She deplored "the outrage of the Missourians" and commented that Harriet Beecher Stowe's *Uncle Tom's Cabin* had produced the most mistaken and often absurd notions of America and American life."[12]

Dix sailed home from Liverpool on September 16, 1856.[13]

In 1857, when the Government Hospital in Washington was complete, Dr. Nichols set aside on the third floor a room for Dix, his close friend for years.[14] Not only had she lobbied to have Nichols administer the building of the hospital, but also to be its first superintendent. He was also her personal physician and financial advisor. And he was perhaps the only person who would have dared tease her to help him find a wife. At that time Dix was fifty-one years old, seventeen years older than Nichols. Her age was guarded by Dix and many believed her to be in her 30's because of her slender frame, excellent posture and beautiful voice. As their friendship deepened, Nichols, in private, began to address Dix as 'Christiana' and 'Angelina' before finally adopting 'Sandora.' In turn, Dix sometimes referred to him as 'St. Nicholas.'[15]

Extensive travels by Dix over several months were described by her in a letter to her friend Annie while Dix was in Nashville: "I do not know whether you have followed my devious journey, but {you can} if you will look on the map for Philadelphia, Baltimore, Washington, Chesapeake Bay, Norfolk, Williamsburg, York, Hampton, Portsmouth, Raleigh, N. Carolina, Weldon, Petersburg, Richmond, Charlottesville, Trenton, Rockbridge, Central Virginia, Salem, Abingdon, Bristol, Virginia, Dalton, Georgia, Chattanooga and Nashville."[16]

Dix: March 9, 1858, Washington: My Dear Sir and Friend, I still find myself too busy to carry out as yet my proposed visit to Virginia, and I fully have in my mind that enjoyment as one of the certain objects to be realized before these matters are passed. I shall indeed feel duly annoyed if anything should occur to hinder this design. I write these lines to keep myself in your remembrance as a promised guest, and with cordial regards to Mrs. Stribling and family and you, Truly in friendly testament, DL Dix."

Dix: May 7, 1858, 917 Chestnut Street, Philadelphia, PA. My Dear Sir, You will think I am a very uncertain person and not reliable in plans or proposed purpose. Since I last wrote, I have been called by the suffering conditions (of those) in the eastern counties of Pennsylvania, and now have been summoned to attest to the death of an old and beloved friend. In regard therefore to my visit at Staunton, I can only say that even if it is delayed till mid-summer, I mean to come and see your family of whom I retain such pleasant recollections, and your hospital in which I have a definite interest. Your friend cordially, DL Dix."

While traveling from Staunton, Virginia to Nashville, Tennessee in the summer of 1858, Dix stopped to visit several of Virginia's Springs. Some were located in the area that became West Virginia after the Civil War. Her experiences as a woman traveling alone are engaging and enlightening, especially coming from one of the most traveled women of her times. Dix complimented and disparaged others. Her enchantment with the beautiful countryside is almost poetic.

Visitors came from Virginia, other states, Europe and other foreign countries. They were drawn by the coolness of the higher elevations in summer and the absence of many deadly diseases prominent in other locations. The mineral content of the waters drew some interested in improving their health. All enjoyed the excellent food and others could chose from a variety of activities: dancing, billiards, pistol galleries, tin-pin alleys, riding horses and carriages for excursions.[17]

An excellent description of the Springs was included in J.J. Morrman's, *Virginia Springs and Springs of the South and West.* Excerpts follow.

> The Springs contained minerals of every variety: various *sulphur* waters, Chalybeates (impregnated with salts of iron) simple and compound; the Aluminous or acidulated aluminous chalybeates, in three or four varieties: and thermal temperatures from 62 to 106 degrees.

> The waters of all of the springs, the Alleghany, the Alum, the Salt, the Red, the Hot, and Healing have their own value. Hence, they all should be described and prescribed intelligently, and used as indicated for a variety of illnesses. Those who came to be cured from illnesses should remain at one Spring long enough to benefit from its waters. A resident doctor should be present to examine the patient and prescribe the most exact water treatment. He should also keep a record of the patient's progress in orders to prescribe safe, certain, and effective remedies for the diseases of future patients.[18]

> Advice for after they returned home follow: Imprudence in eating and drinking should be carefully avoided, especially because the minerals often sharpened the appetite and digestion. Other excesses should be avoided; for example, staying up late; prolonged and immoderate dancing, remaining too long in the cool air of evening. Passions should be kept in check by avoiding either too much excitement or, in contrast, melancholy. A giddy chase after pleasure and luxurious indulgence was not needed; nor indolence and seclusion. Exercise, adjusted for the patient, was also beneficial.[19]

Dix: Rockbridge Alum, (Date, 1858 month unknown) My Dear Sir and Friend, I arrived here without accident, enjoying the stage drive greatly over the mountain. Why did no one tell me of the fair vistas which are but a journey over the . . . . Those Blue Mountains, magnificent and breathless forests, and the . . . located in beautiful streams, sparkling cascades at . . . Springs. Then the varied types of forest trees and the lovely flowering plants, and shrubs. Tis truly a very attractive country and I shall recommend my friends who are lovers of the grand and beautiful to see these up close.

This place is special and certainly offers some unusually pleasant features apart from the tour up close. I don't know how much one might become interested in studying character here, there is a great variety. I have already seen some cheerful, amiable persons. A lady from Georgia, my nearest neighbor at once, treated me kindly, and at the same appreciated I was a stranger alone and having the appearance of an invalid. Dr. Frazier was at once the courteous landlord, and I, as at your most hospitable house, find the inclination to linger strong and not easy to throw aside. But I shall proceed today (to) the Warm and perhaps the Hot Springs, according to conveyance and availability. I doubt often I was in the cars that the committee had determined the location of the new hospital not far from Parkersburg. I think I am near Weston, with that location of knowledge and wisdom still to be shown.

I think without doubt I shall cross the country to strike the Tennessee (local) path. Probably, I shall write several times before I reach Nashville. I must take leave again expressing my sense of your . . . kind care for entire satisfaction in visiting your hospital and for the great kindness that surrounded me in the pleasant Stribling family circle. I send a kiss to Hettie by her Mama, and good wishes to Master Frank.

I am charmed by the tinkling cowbells because they bring me by association to the lovely Alps and Tyrolean Highlands in Europe. Yet there is no great music in a cowbell! Your friend with cordial and regards to Mrs. Stribling, the daughters and . . . little girl and wishes for the little baby. DL Dix (It appears that the Stribling's were now grandparents.)

Dix: July 4, 1858, White Sulfur Springs, Sunday Evening, My Dear Sir and Friend, I arrived here late yesterday at twelve, intending fully to proceed enroute for the Tennessee RR at least 5 miles, to pass Sunday in a more congenial place if one could be found in a reasonable distance. It {the Springs} might perhaps be considered rather desirable than otherwise to people from the lower Mississippi plantations or the Mississippi region. But any person used to the ordinary comforts, not to say, . . . of ordinary life in the main, should come here to spend a week, much less months . . . and . . . quite uncomfortable. The Rock Alum is very pleasant and the Bath Alum very comfortable, though both are without accommodations of baths.

That Hot Springs being comfortless, are badly kept, the baths bad and inconsistent: the All-Healing really charming. The Warm Springs being desirable are both pleasant and comfortable. But the White Sulfur is boiling, but totally disgusting. It has a spring of pure water and some beautiful trees, and one sees finely wooded mountains that are made valueless at present by the surroundings.

I took a (stagecoach) from the Alum and went to the top of the Warm Springs . . . while the stage was reaching end and finding its way up the long ascent what a grand view is had from the stagecoach. There I dipped into the beautiful Warm Spring bath, happily no people yet there. (I do not see how they manage with only two resources for all the bathers.) and then took the stage to the Hot Springs and was very glad to get off before breakfast; the next day to the Warm Springs All-Healing, where the . . . delay of the stage for six hours gave me time . . . and to explore a lovely gorge and valley and see Fortes . . . Cascades and Falls which were very fine . . . ferns (known) and trees as well as the . . . are beautiful.

Dix: July 6,1858, Salem: Dear Friend, I cannot recall if I asked you to send mail to me at Nashville for . . . Place Station, the cars today stopping a day at Knoxville. The only line of cars Tuesday reaches Abingdon past midnight and leaves at the same hour. This will break two nights if I stop for a day as I wished. I am hesitating because I do not feel strong and not as well as when I left your hospitable house. I have no words to express the delight and full enjoyment I have had of the trees and the mountains. I am pleased with the Rockbridge Bath Alum, Warm, All Healing, Little Red, Roanoke Red, crows and mountaintops. I am not with the . . . much—not at all with the White Sulfur except several fine views from the hills . . . and those are very fine.

Taylor, the gambler from Washington, had leased the use and control of the gambling tables at the White Sulphur for ten thousand dollars for the season, including the exclusive right to sell cigars.

My love to all your family. I have much to tell you of this charming country. But no time now. If I feel better, I will stop at Abingdon, if I cannot, the cars and stages have changed hands so much lately that it is not easy to make any plans, including . . . Your friend, DL Dix.

Dix: Probably July 1858, White Sulfur Springs . . . Proceeded . . . to (Calabasas) which is . . . situated in fine country . . . and surrounded by abrupt hills. The house bitterly comfortless! Should I ever find myself in these parts again, I shall try a neat little farmhouse nearby that looked quite interesting.

Yesterday, a lady was drowned in the Ladies Reservoir . . . at the Red Sulfur. I have only heard this sad fact by descriptions. It is not possible to say when I shall reach Nashville as I am quite at the mercy of stage agents who staff its coaches and send them on according to their own pleasure at present. Our agent assured me that I should certainly not be discharged at this place. And if I had asked to see the country . . . . I could do so by proceeding thither from Calabasas and taking the other coach which runs regularly to Balzac's. After I had been here an hour and a half, they concluded not to go until Monday.

I sincerely hope my 'living' house will not be announced elsewhere, as it often is; needlessly. I would feel very much mortified. I will write to you from Nashville, but from what I can learn, I do not think I shall reach there before Thursday.

I saw yesterday in a paper that a stage goes daily from Staunton to Stribling Springs. If I had known this, I certainly would have gone there. I like to see what these places offer, and the Springs there are worth seeing in all this country. A lovely country it is indeed. I shall always remember its fine natural beauties. And often wish to see again those grand chains of mountains . . . which is truly a blessing to have.

I must tell you before I close this letter that I am much satisfied in recollecting your hospital as affording many comforts and making steady improvements, Tis a great satisfaction to have this.

My kind regards to Mrs. Stribling and all the family, if you please. I hope that you received the letter I sent from the Rockbridge Alum, but that it was very valuable, but I had promised to write, and would but have you think I forget your report. Your friend with respect and friendly wishes. DL Dix.

PS—Should you have any thing forward, please forward to Clarksville.

Where new hospitals were being contemplated or being built, Dix described her successes and frustrations with state legislators. She also shared with Stribling information that she was constantly receiving through her extensive correspondence with doctors and politicians nationwide.

Dix wrote to Stribling shortly after she reached Nashville. After describing traveling difficulties, she gossiped about Dr. Fisher of North Carolina, chided Stribling because he had not written and described the activities of several hospitals north of Virginia.

Dix: July 15, 1858, Tennessee State Hospital for the Insane, Nashville, My Dear Sir and Friend:

After a variety of experiences, I reached Nashville early Sunday after obliged to travel all night or be detained for two days, which I was not willing to subject myself to a 'chance tavern' en route. The hospital is doing better than I could hardly have expected, and reflects great credit on Dr. Chatham.

I had a long letter by the last post from Dr. Fisher. He speaks of his lady as again indisposed. And I shall not be surprised if he already is in the East for his favorite summer resort at an all-healing Spring. He sighs for the peace of . . . . I think he should (have) considered the mountains, for Eastern Virginia has nothing to boast of pure treatment as my latest recollections show. I shall never cease to enjoy the recollections of your fine mountain views, and of their noble forests, with their fine springs which have been . . . for coloring and the beautiful clouds floating . . . . hours over and around the mountain tops.

I am hoping to hear from you by today's post. I will, by the eighth, expect to meet the trustees of this institution, and as I cannot reach each hospital with those of two days from hence, must defer departure to Monday next. Thence to Louisville and Lexington. At the latter place, letters will find me addressed in care of Dr. Chefley.

I have not a line from you since I left Staunton, but this is my loss though, not being able to give you my address. I learned in the Cars that Governor Campbell was not in Abingdon and that decided me, as I passed the place on a dark stormy night . . . . at about two in the morning, not to delay there. Though I had previously questioned the propriety of the place, as I should have been obliged to leave by journeying again in the night. And finally on Sunday could find me leave early for Nashville. But advanced by the "Georgia Line,' I should find too much loss of time.

I have just had good news of hospital affairs from Trenton, Utica, Philadelphia, Harrisburg, and D.C. Dr. "C" has a gardener who quite rivals your excellent collection. I think you both very fortunate. I desire most cordial regards to all in the Stribling family circle and remembrances at the hospital. Your friend with respect and high affection, DL Dix.

On July 23, 1858, Stribling finally answered several letters that he had received from Dix. He also described a visit by Dr. Jones, updated Dix on the new hospital that had been proposed in Virginia and described preparations made by the Governor of Virginia to greet Dix at Abingdon, but she had not stopped. Stribling also apologized to Dix that he had not suggested that she visit Stribling Springs.

Stribling: July 23, 1858, Staunton, Va., My Dear Miss Dix, Your recent favors were only received and highly valued. They came respectively from Rockbridge Alum, White Sulfur, Salem and Nashville, the later reached (me) here by last mail. Some few days after you left us, I was unexpectedly called to Richmond, and was absent from my post three days. On my return, I found the letters from you which were forwarded to Nashville, and acknowledged in your last letter. But I also found that my official duties had, in that brief period, so accumulated as to preclude me from dropping you a line.

I have deferred writing, because of the probability that if my letter should go to Nashville, it would have to be forwarded, and I preferred sending it directly to the point where it would meet you. In your last letter, you gave me to understand that this one will meet you at Lexington, KY.

I know not where to begin in giving you details as to occurrences since you left us, but will first say that your friend, Dr. Jones, arrived here on the morning of the 6th. He found me waiting by the afternoon train, the . . . of my Dear Old Father, of whose illness you heard me speak. I introduced Dr. Jones to Doctors Hamilton and Davis and asked for him, their kindest attention. At nine o'clock that night, I received the dispatch which called me to Richmond, and considered to leave by the cars early in the morning of the seventh, and without again seeing Dr. Jones, but hoping to meet with him. On my return, I found that he had passed much of his time in the asylum that produced a most favorable impression as to his intelligence and gentlemanly bearing. He had by special invitation spent an evening at my residence.

He left Staunton the morning after I reached home, but without calling upon me. Had I known he was thinking of going so soon, fatigued as I was, I should have visited him. I understood that his report was hurried by the assignment that he had received the appointment of superintendent to Dr. Nichols.

You doubtless feel much interest in regard to our Trans-Allegheny Asylum (Northwestern) and I am truly glad to inform you that thus far, matters are encouraging. From what I can learn from acquaintances, the commissioners have made a fortunate selection of a site. I send herewith an extract from a Petersburg paper (prepared I doubt not, by one of the commissioners) which will give you some idea of the place. The character of the land, the accessibility of the place, the water advantages are said to be unusual. But the coal on the land, which will almost be free of cost for material to furnish fuel and lights, is a feature of which no institution can boast.

As to the construction and organization of the establishment, I think the board of directors appointed since the site was located are disposed to act cautiously and deliberately. I have received letters informing me that the plan of buildings would be submitted to me for endorsement, asking for suggestions. I send you a copy of the last letter which I have written in response upon the subject, and doubtless you will at least agree with me on the appointment of a physician before any other step is taken. This, I apprehend, is a step which the Board was not prepared. The matter should be submitted to the Governor for his advice. If you approve, a letter from you to Governor Wise may do much good! You will, if you write, have to do so speedily as the Governor is a 'quick' man.

I send also a letter from Governor Campbell. You will perceive that the old gentlemen had not only made arrangements, but also had planned for your reception and safe keeping at the depot. He was prepared to give you a cordial and hospitable welcome. I regret much that you did not stop at Abingdon, but of course, appreciate the reasons given in your last letter.

I received a letter from Miss D. A. Lloyd of Philadelphia, apparently in response to a communication from you, saying that there were two young ladies under her care, one or the other of who might suit Miss Campbell, asking for information as to the requisite issues. This letter I forwarded to Governor Campbell. At the same time, I gave him the apology for your not stopping at Abingdon which you furnished in advance, thus your letter from Salem. I also wrote Miss Lloyd, saying that Governor would correspond with her should he still desire a companion for his Lady.

We are getting on much as usual at this large and somewhat unwieldy establishment. Your visit created quite an impression, and its reoccurrence at short intervals would, I know, be valued by many beside me. How much I should wish that we could so divide our large, established building for . . . finally, as to make six instead of three classes, and consequently have twelve, instead of six, attendants at each! But this, I fear is impracticable. The division in the corresponding building for males, will, I trust, be made before the winter. The chests for clothing and as seats will not be forgotten.

Miss Tinsley, has this moment entered my office, and asks to be kindly remembered. Says she is sure your visit did us proud.

We were truly pleased to learn that you so much enjoyed the scenery in Marion, Virginia. Having been born and raised in the mountains, we are naturally not so much aware of their beauty as one less accustomed. This must be our excuse for not having made more effort to excite your curiosity in regard to the mountains, valleys, forests, and mineral waters. The truth is that none of us thought of this 'noble' place when you were with us, or finally, you would have been urged to visit it.

My family are each as well as when you left us. You know not what an impression you have left upon my dear wife. She repeats that, if afflicted and needing a peculiar friend, she wishes to be the protegee of Miss Dix.

We have with us now the daughters of Bishop Johns, most cultured and interesting ladies. You would, I know, be pleased with them, and they express much regret at your departing before they arrived. My daughters are well, Frank is making a visit to Fauquier and Clarke Counties and seems to be enjoying his visit greatly. All at home wish to be affectionately remembered.

I request that you make allowances in the abrupt manner in which this is written. But, it is, I fear, you would think me somewhat ironical, in view of the fact that I must say it be read more easily than any production letters which it has been my pleasure to receive from you. With my best wishes and hoping soon again to hear from you, I remain most truly your friend, Fran. T. Stribling.

PS—I omitted to state that I had a visit from Dr. Parker of Columbia, SC last week. He spent several days with me and is a very pleasant gentleman. He asked particularly of you and desires much that you make him a visit.

Dix: Thursday, probably 1858

I have just arrived here from Raleigh, NC and proceed hence for Staunton on Saturday morning.

Yours with best regards to all the family. DL Dix

Stribling: January 11, 1859, Staunton, Va., My Dear Miss Dix, Your esteemed favor of 6th inst. was duly received. A box containing the stereoscope and bin reached us yesterday. It also contained all the articles of 'The American Sunday School Union' except the map on Jerusalem. This map, the prints and engravings from Earle of Philadelphia, the lot of pictures from New York, the Horticulture Journal, will I dare say, arrive in due time. Should there be any unusual delay, I will write you.

I am gratified that you purchased the stereoscope. The instrument seems a good one and the views are handsome. With proper regulations, it can be made interesting and useful to all, especially to such as could not attend exhibitions with the magic lanterns.

If I understand your letter, excuse me for saying that as to your figures at hand, it is difficult to decipher! Our account stands as follows.

The asylum is charged

Account	80.00
Earles	75.48
N.Y. purchase-pictures	52.00
American Sunday school Union	17.00
Horticulture Journal	1.00
	$225.48
Is credited—with check on Valley Bank	$200.00
Balance due Miss Dix	25.48

We cheerfully send a check for this balance, and by that you will feel not the slightest delicacy in suggesting any mistake in the above statement. I intend ordering two of the airbeds of which Dr. Kirkbride writes you, but would prefer the waterbed if it be had. I am pleased you are visiting our friend, Dr. Fisher. He will give you doubtless a hearty welcome. Please present me to him and Mrs. Fisher, in the kindest form.

My family is well except little Hettie, who is not seriously sick. All asked to be affectionately remembered to you. In much haste and truly yours, Fran. T. Stribling.

Shadows of dark slaves hovered unspoken over Dix and Stribling for years. Stribling not only owned personal slaves but also rented others to do menial work at Western State.

Dix had been appalled when she first observed slavery in 1830 on a trip with the Channing family to St. Croix. Her strong reaction was expressed in a letter to Mrs. Torrey.

> "Disguise thyself as thou wilt, still slavery, thou art a bitter draught and human nature will not wear thy chains without cursing the ground for the enslaver's sake . . . . sure I am that retribution will fall on the slave-merchant, the slaveholder, and their children until the fourth generation.[20]

Later, another impassioned comment on slavery was made by Dix. "These beings, slave owners, I repeat, *cannot be Christians*, they cannot act as moral beings, and they cannot act as souls destined for immortality. No path, no good, can follow in the path trodden by slavery."[21]

Years later however when Dix prepared to take her crusade to build institutions for the insane in the South, she faced a dilemma. She did not want 'abolitionist' to be added to her burden of being a 'Yankee' and 'woman.' If defined that way, her crusade in the South could be damaged. Therefore, when Dix was forced to choose between helping the insane in the South or supporting the blacks in the North, she chose the insane and remained silent on slavery.

Even though they shared their thoughts on every conceivable subject, slavery was not mentioned in their letters for years, and probably not in person. Perhaps Dix thought it would be rude to do so as a guest in the Stribling household in close quarters surrounded by his personal slaves. Dix surely would have been uncomfortable being waited on by slaves. And she could not help but notice the hired slaves doing menial work at Western State on her frequent visits there.

And why had Stribling not raised the subject? Were both of them uncertain whether or not their friendship could survive such a discussion?

Finally, in a letter to Stribling in early 1859, Dix questioned Western State's policy on admitting insane blacks. Because of her frequent trips to Eastern State, whose policy was to admit blacks, she may have assumed that Western State did the same.

Later, Dix congratulated Stribling on his recent raise in salary and plans for the new hospital for the insane in Virginia.

Stribling: March 12, 1859, Staunton, Va. My Dear Miss Dix, Your esteemed letter returned from . . . was only received, and I had no idea until looking over my bunch of unanswered letters this morning, that I had been tardy in returning you my sincere thanks for it. What you heard in Raleigh as to the increase in my salary was, I am glad to say, correct. It was on the first of January raised to $3500, and I shall feel, you may be assured, not the slightest delicacy in taking every cent. I believe that anyone occupying my position, if he discharges his duties, earns the salary.

You were misinformed as to Dr. Kirkbride's and myself having committed to examine and modify the plans prepared by J. Imboden Andrews for the buildings at Weston. We were requested to do so by the board of directors, and my position was so peculiar, that after solicitation, I could not feel free to deny the request. We were asked only for our views as to the buildings; not a syllable about the location.

After examining the plans, we presented the results of our actions in a report to the directors, and we were very careful, as neither of us had ever visited the place, and knew nothing personally of the land or the advantages thus afforded for such an establishment, made no allusion to the institution. The plan agreed and advised on, the architect informs us, could not be placed on the land now belonging to the institution. But he wrote that there was land adjacent which the owner refused to sell, and which the directors designed, applying to the next legislature for authority to have it condemned.

This must, of course, attract attention and cause the inquiry (as to) why that in a body of 300 and more acres already purchased, there cannot be found sufficient space for 250 patients. This will be the good time for anyone who may design opposing the location of the contemplated establishment at that place to do so. I am, of course, so delicately situated that it would be improper for me to volunteer any opinion in the premises. I fully agree with you, however, that the State had far better lose $25,000 than to spend $200,000 to $250,000 in building an institution, which when completed, would fail in its humane desires.

All of your purchases came safely except the Map of Jerusalem. The express company is in search for it and say, if not found, they will make it good. I purchased sundry articles, including a considerable addition to the library for entertainment, and (to) promote the exercise of my patients. I am also negotiating for a good billiard table which we think will be useful.

In most inputs, we are getting along here about as when you last looked in upon us. In reply to your question, I have to say that there never was but one insane Negro, she free, in this institution, and that many years ago. Both free blacks and slaves are received at Williamsburg, but I am unable to give you information as to the numbers.

Some years since, I urged upon the legislature the importance of providing for this class of insane, and suggested that this might be done in connection with one or both of the hospitals for whites providing the buildings were so detached, I should say isolated, so that whilst the two classes might be supervised and attended by the same medical officers, steward, and matron, in all other respects they should appear as distinct, and separate establishments. But I expressed a decided preference that an institution for the colored insane should in all respects be . . . and maintained my warm thoughts.

Dr. Galt, however, at the same time, reported that such patients could easily be provided for at Eastern Hospital Asylum without additional expenditures for buildings and, as a matter of course the legislature, always unwilling to appropriate money if to be avoided, adopted Galt's plan. Since then many have, I know, been sent to his care.

I trust you have passed a pleasant winter and found much to interest you in the South. The papers informed us that you are highly delighted with Dr. Green's hospital in Georgia that promises in all respects, to become the best in the South. I can but congratulate Dr. Green on receiving such a compliment.

My family is as usual. My poor wife has suffered much at times during the winter but has rallied and is now quite comfortable. Fanny will leave us on Monday for Norfolk and spend some time with her friends. Ella will be following after a while. We will, of course, miss them very much. Frank is well and busy with his books, and little Hettie is very well and sprightly. She conceived quite a desire to learn to read and is really making considerable progress. All unite in thanks for your kind messages, and ask to be affectionately remembered. Wishing you a prolonged life, health, and happiness. Your kind friend truly, Frans. T.Stribling.

Note: No person in Virginia had worked harder to have an institution built in Virginia for the black insane. Over several years he and his directors broached the subject to the legislature, and Stribling even presented a plan for it. Years later, those involved in creating Central State Hospital for blacks reported that they had referred to Stribling's plan for guidance.

It is interesting that Dix felt it necessary to clarify her comments about the effectiveness of various hospitals. Her letter also confirms her involvement in all aspects of hospital design and construction.

Dix: Incomplete and undated letter to Stribling.

. . . Education is making good progress in all the most settled parts of Texas, which was a wonderful country. You certainly could not believe that I ever thought or said what is inputted to me concerning the Georgia hospital. One could not help that which people, sometimes for interest and reasons, ascribed to one. I rank the five South-line states together: South Carolina, Georgia, Alabama, Louisiana, and Mississippi. Of those, I perhaps may have remarked that, at present, Georgia had in occupation, the best buildings and height to make it in a few years a first-class institution 'with diligent care.'

I should not dream of ranking it with yours, with that at Lexington or the Nashville institution. I have really been exceedingly cautious in expressing any opinions at all, except to your superintendents who are my confidential friends, and to whom I say candidly many things I should not utter to others.

In regard to hospital architecture, I feel increasingly convinced that construction should be studied, with regard to adaptation to climate; this has, I fear, been too much overlooked. A plan extremely well-suited to Massachusetts or Pennsylvania is not adapted to South Carolina or Alabama. And in the latter instance, while the plan hardly . . . . if built upon in Canada, is singularly in fault in a hot climate where it is constructed . . . verandas, corridors and windows should be multiplied.

Please give my love and affectionate regards to Mrs. Stribling and your daughters. Kind regards to acquaintances in the hospital, and recollect me as friend with respect, esteem, and cordial friendship. DL Dix.

I go to Jackson, Louisiana Delta, Mississippi, (and) St. Joseph, Missouri and next to St. Louis. If you write to the latter places, please direct them to the . . . .

In the following letter Dix again chides Stribling for not writing more often and demands that if he does not have time to write, then one of the Stribling daughters should. She also seems somewhat sad that her friendships were not flourishing.

Dix: November 22, 1859, Jackson, Mississippi, My Dear Sir and Friend. The best greetings to yourself and family! It has been so long since I heard from you, that I cannot go back to the date. Many times since, I have intended to write, express myself, and ask of your affairs. But crowding duties and consequent . . . of time have taken me off friends, and though with often thoughts of them, I have had no written communications.

Will you have one of the daughters write to me at once, addressing it to Columbia, South Carolina where I am obliged to go directly. And I hope to find the legislature there in a spirit of liberal activity, although their very short sessions, three weeks from the twenty-seventh to the thirty-first. At present, exacting political and social questions do not encourage the idea that much will be done, beyond setting the attention more definitely on the question of improving the state institution.

Dr. Parker writes that he is constantly refusing patients for lack of room. And I suppose there are hundreds in any state who ought to be subjects of hospital protection and medical treatment, but who do not come within the institutions at all. As a whole, impartiality is shown in his hospital. But it seems to me now, by such external things than defined in hindsight, whether really much thought is employed upon the manifestations and causes of mental ailments, is a question that I think might be considered with profit. One reason for this lapse, no doubt, can be found in institutions accounting a more consistent oversight, increased responsibility, and mutual intent with those who stood at the head of affairs, should be sought. In fact, leisure for thought and study in real time for relaxation, are almost unknown. Those who focus take losses which delay by some other . . . and . . . . abuses. Am I correct in this summary?

I must write and answer, first expressing most cordial regards to Mrs. Stribling and the family. Your friend, DL Dix.

A letter that Stribling wrote to Dix in the late fall of 1859 is missing because she refers to it in her following letter. In a plaintive tone, she expresses her need to be with the Stribling Family, writing that "a visit would affect both heart and mind."

Dix: December 9, 1859, Columbia, S.C., My Dear Sir and Friend: I have just received your letter and am glad you can support our bill and am hopeful. I regret that in general well being, my friend, Mrs. Stribling has shared less largely than some. Please give her my love and best wishes with considerable regards to her and the daughters. I am pleased that dear Frank and Hettie recalled me so handily. And that they are growing strong and well. I wish I could afford a few days to be with you all. It would affect both heart and mind. For some matters certainly, I cannot.

Decidedly, I agree that there could be but one head over an institution for the insane, anymore than one captain over a ship or head of an army. But I think surely something must be done to improve the home life of patients.

I shall go to Tennessee if in two short weeks I can be of use at all to Dr. Chatham. And at his request, February belongs to . . . . The Tennessee legislature reorganized after the 10th. They must have their say, either an exhibition, or bury the hospital! I should be going to a . . . . as they propose on the adjacent farm. I don't like the division of taxes. The family life should have its share, at least within an institution for the insane, if it is to enjoy the social and domestic relations in reality.

I should like a long table on hospital affairs. Thank you for your hospital report. Please send a copy to Doctor J.D. Stewart, Esq., supervisor, in Jackson, Miss. and one to Doctor {Weller} Hospital Lab No. 1, and Dr. Frank Patterson in Augusta. I wish you had the right sort of assistant in your chemical department.

Purposefully and . . . . Your friend, DL Dix

Nearly a year later Dix wrote Stribling the following that gives us some insight as to her views on the upcoming Civil War. It also confirms the affection that Stribling's peer doctors in the North, in spite of political differences, wanted to visit him.

Dix: November 26, 1860, Philadelphia, My Dear Sir and Friend, It must be a good while since I have written to you and your family of my friendly and affectionate remembrances. Not the less have I held you in sincere regard, but my very occupied life spares me little time for 'those demonstrations of intent that keep the chain bright,' and I rest in the faith my friends have in my steadfastness more than rely on repetitive expressions of attachment.

And I have not long since returned from the western states which I have been engaged in describing all the conditions of the poor and needy, the insane and helpless. For a short time I pursued those same objects in the middle states. I had hoped strongly that I could see you all early this past autumn,

Our . . . . friends, "The Muted Brethren," as I call the hospital superintendents in general, prosper and guide their affairs with discretion and zeal to successful results. A remarkable chapter of health had pervaded the conventional hospitals and the country the past year except in Illinois where scarlet fever had been a scourge, and I only have received vague reports from Kentucky.

Doctors Brown, Buttolph, Kirkbride and Nichols from time to time tried to engage in visits to you, but one or the other always had been prevented from leaving home at the planned time. And winter has come without the realization of their plans.

The disturbed state of public affairs in the country at this junction, is calculated to fill every good and reflecting soul with great regret. If self-seeking politicians and disaffected aspirants were not so busy in fermenting discord and opening breeches, there would be cause for solicitude on every hand. One could only hope that their weakness and folly would come to an end before serious mischiefs befall.

My love to Mrs. Stribling and all at home. Your excellent friend with cordial regards and respect. DL Dix

The following note was written by someone for Dix. That note and the 1874 letter following it confirm that Dix and Stribling resumed their friendship after the Civil War ended. And she was still shopping for him. It is very probable that missing correspondence between them exists.

Washington D.C. January, 1871

Miss Dix reportedly acknowledges receipt of Dr. Stribling's report upon the Central State Hospital for the Insane of Virginia for 1870. It is interesting that after so much time, Dix is still shopping for Stribling.

Dix: January or February 17, 1874.

Dear Sir:

Yours was here upon my return from Maryland. I send by express eighteen lithographic prints and two pieces of music which may interest some of your patients. Also pictures in glass for your stereopticon together with a catalogue of Brewer's collection at his Rooms in Philadelphia. Some of his subjects are really good, and yet, I hardly think effective enough to entertain most of your patients. I think his prices are moderate, 1$ each.

The statuary carries out too hard for general exhibition to suit my taste. When I have opportunity in March or April, I hope to select something for stereoscopes which will be of interest. I can get nothing in Washington at this time that is desirable.

Doctor and Mrs. Nichols are well (and) would send friendly greetings if they knew I was writing.

I ask remembrance to your family and of Dr. and Mrs. Fisher. I am sorry to learn that Mrs. Fisher suffers from ill health.

Your friend D.L. Dix

DIX–DURING AND AFTER THE CIVIL WAR

On April 23, 1861 Secretary of War Simon Cameron accepted Dix's offer to serve the Union by issuing the following order:

> Be it known to all who are concerned that the free services of Miss D. L. Dix are accepted by the War Department: and that she will give at all times. all necessary aid in organizing Military Hospitals, for the care of all of the sick and wounded soldiers, aiding the Chief Surgeon by supplying nurses and substantial means for the comfort and relief of the suffering; also that she is fully authorized to receive, control, and disburse special supplies bestowed by individuals or associations for the comfort of their friends or the citizen soldiers from all parts of the United States, as also under sanction of the Acting Surgeon General to draw from the Army stores.[1]

On June 10, 1861, Dix was commissioned Superintendent of all of the Female Nurses of the Army, the first in American history. In that position, Dorothea Dix had more authority and power in the nation that any other woman ever held.[2]

Dix immediately began work, writing that "no woman under thirty need apply to serve in Government Hospitals. All nurses are to be plain looking. Their dresses must be brown or black, with no bows, no curls, no jewelry, and no hoop skirts."[3] Volunteers were to remain home until Dix summoned them.[4]

The nurses were also to be "sober, earnest, self-sacrificing, and self-contained who can bear the presence of suffering and exercise entire self control of speech and manner, who can be calm, gentle, quiet, active and steadfast in duty, and willing to take and exercise the directions of the surgeons."[5] As the war continued and the wounded increased, Dix was unable to maintain those restrictions.

Dix protected her nurses as they labored in brutal environments and she was also concerned about the ill soldiers there to whom they ministered. She provided a house in Washington where nurses could rest during their infrequent leaves from duty.[6]

Dix refused to be cowed by the military bureaucracy and frequently clashed with them. Those she would associate with during the war were passionate either in admiring or despising Dix. One doctor wrote that she was 'a very retiring, sensitive woman, yet brave and bold as a lion to do battle for the right and for justice . . . [7] Samuel Gridley wrote in 1861, "Miss Dix who is the terror of all mere formalists, idlers and evil-doers goes there {hospitals} as she goes everywhere to prevent and remedy abuses and shortcomings."[8]

Some called her "Dragon Dix" because she was stern and brusque. "Miss Dix has plagued us a little." wrote George Templeton Strong, a member of the United Sanitation Commission, a private relief agency. "She is energetic, benevolent, and a mild case of monomania. Working on her own hook, she does good, but no one can cooperate with her for she belongs to the class of comets and can be subdued into relations with no system whatever."[9]

Surgeons and hospital administrators complained to the Surgeon General about her prying and poking about. Over time, her authority was reduced and her influence eroded.[10] Still Dix had her admirers, among them the soldiers she visited and important persons in the Government. After the war ended, Secretary of War Edwin M. Stanton awarded her two national flags for 'the Care, Succor and Relief of the sick and wounded Soldiers of the United States on the Battle-Field, in Camps and Hospitals during the recent War.'[11]

To her credit, Dix did not forget her former friends from the South. One example was her efforts to help young Frank Stribling after she discovered that he was a prisoner of war. Stribling wrote two letters to Dix, obviously in reply to correspondence that he received from her. She also may have influenced the transmission of letters between young Stribling and his family. His unedited letters to Dix follow.

December 17, 1864

> Your note has just been handed me and I hasten to reply. I am much obliged for your kind offer to supply my wants. I am glad to be able to report myself quite comfortable and in want of nothing at present. Since my imprisonment I have suffered occasionally from Dyspepsia—with that exception I am very well. I should like much to be able to receive a box of eatable, but no permits of any kind is being granted. The rations, altho quite sufficient, do not agree with me.If you could obtain a permit for me, I would be under lasting obligations. Should you have an opportunity of sending a letter to my parents, be so kind as to tell them where and how I am—that I wrote per last flag of truce in October and also put a personal ad in the New York Times a few weeks since. My cousin Mr. Spencer of Baltimore has kindly sent me money. If you can spare time from your arduous duties, I will be much pleased to hear from you again. Address as above, care of Major A. G. Brady. Very respectfully yours, FT. Stribling, Jr.[12]

On January 17, 1865, Stribling wrote Dix again. By now he was feeling the strains of imprisonment.

> Yours of the 21st of January has just been received. I was glad to hear from home tonight. Mrs. Stribling and I are much obliged to you for writing me. I received two letters from home by the last truce boat. I enclose you one. Since I last wrote you my health has not been good, although I have taken particular care of myself. My eyesight which has always been very imperfect has failed me much since my confinement. Presuming upon the intimacy existing between my father and yourself, may I not ask you to use your influence in getting me exchanged on one of the boats which are now running for that purpose. My constitution you remember has always been delicate. I fear nobody on myself but on my parents who are extremely anxious about me. Will you be so kind as to aid me? It would give me much pleasure to hear from you again. Be so kind as to give Mrs. Stribling my address and ask her to write me. Your friend truly, F.T. Stribling, Jr.[13]

Mrs. Henrietta Stribling wrote to her son Frank on December 1, 1864. This is the only letter written by Mrs. Stribling that has surfaced.

Your letter, my dear child, was received about ten days ago. I was rejoiced once more to see your handwriting, telling me you were well. I am tolerably comfortable, and since then have seen Mr. B. who was exchanged. He told me that he left you and Ranson some little articles that he had collected for his comfort, such as a stove that I hope you may find useful to you as long as you stay.

I trust in the course of events that you will soon be exchanged; your youth and delicate constitution will no doubt be in your favor. I hope that you will observe all the rules laid down for the prisoners and thus get on quietly. Mr. B said that you had a prospect of getting a place left by T. Hammond's exchange. I hope you did, as then you will have some employment and less exposure, as I understood it. R. Phillips tells me an exchanged prisoner brings the news of your being in the hospital sick, and that has made me anxious.

Write and tell me how you are. I heard you had a daily prayer meeting that I hope you enjoy and attend. For if we have access to our blessed Savior, we may be happy, even in captivity. The pleasures of the world are worth but little compared with the peace that our Father gives his trusting children for Christ's sake. My longing desire is to meet you in heaven and I see you walking and living very near to Jesus. For this and my daily prayers ascend, and we meet in spirit, often I hope. Sunday is our communion, and how I shall long to have you at my side. But before long, we shall, by the power of God, if you continue to love and serve him, sit down in our Father's kingdom.

Your friends and relations all are well. Fannie will move to Roanoke in a week or two. They have rented a house there for the winter. She was quite sick, and now is better. I sent Betsy to help her move and fix her house. Ella talks of going down after Christmas. I wish we could all be together then. Have you gotten letters from any of our friends in the North? Let us know. Your father is at the asylum all the time, with 300 of the insane to take care of. May the Lord reward his labors. Have you an overcoat? Let me know. We have written twice. Did you get the letters? Your dear mother.[14]

By temperament and experience, Dix was unsuited to being part of a military environment. Still, she worked tirelessly to exercise her duties. She completed all of them before returning to her former life. Immediately, she began to raise money to build a Soldiers' Monument at the National Cemetery in Hampton, Virginia. As usual, Dix was involved in every detail of the project, selecting the granite for the memorial and designing a fence to enclose it made out of muskets. The cornerstone was laid on October 3, 1867.[15]

Treatment of the insane had greatly deteriorated during the war. By the time Dix resumed her efforts to help them, she remarked, "It would seem that all my work is to be done over."[16] Complicating her efforts to help them was a vastly different political environment. Few funds were available to erect enough buildings and hire enough people to accommodate the ever-increasing insane population because the war had drained the country's resources.

Moreover, some of the most highly respected doctors in the field were presenting conflicting solutions on appropriate policies and practices. Among them Doctor Pliny Earle who asserted that insanity was becoming more and more an incurable disease.[17] Doctor William Hammond was especially critical, questioned credentials of some of the superintendents, suggesting that sequestering patients was often unnecessary, even injurious to them; and accusing some superintendents of exaggerating the numbers of cures that they were effecting.[18] Dr. Edward Jarvis and others also recommended that the mildly insane be treated at home.[19]

The comments and suggestions of those doctors were in conflict with some of the basic tenets of moral therapy that had been recommended by the Superintendents Association and Dix for years. Especially scalding to Dix was Hammond's accusation that some of the superintendents had fudged their numbers because many of them were her close friends. Yet, regardless of how the disputes would be resolved, there was much work for Dix to pursue. Once again she began to travel throughout the country, lobbying for more hospitals, evaluating their possible location, and recommending candidates to supervise them. These were conditions she could change; even though Dix had lost some of her influence, her notoriety and authority remained undiminished.

What had not changed was the consuming desire that Dix had held to be a member of a family. For years before the War, that need had been filled by the Striblings. But its members had changed and her former place among them no longer existed. They would have remembered how much Dix helped young Frank Stribling. Because of the many acquaintances they had in common, Dix would have been aware of Stribling's death. At that time had she traveled to Staunton to console Mrs. Stribling and his now adult children? Had she corresponded with them in the years that followed? There is no record that she did either, but she may have.

Nevertheless, the need to be an active member of a family, preferably one with members of varying ages, including children, was still there. Eventually, that yearning was filled by the extensive George Emerson Family that would remain faithful to Dix.[20]

By the time Dix was seventy-six years old, she had lost to death her brother Joseph and several friends, among them Anne Heath.[21] Her own health was gradually deteriorating, and in 1881, she left her quarters at the Government Hospital in Washington and moved to the New Jersey Hospital in Trenton, the hospital Dix had always referred to as 'her first child.' A top-floor suite had been reserved there for Dix since the hospital opened.[22]

There can be little doubt that the independent Dix, surrounded by people all of her life, would have had trouble adjusting to her new surroundings. So it is not surprising that Dix wrote that she often felt 'a vivid sense of aloneness in the hospital.' To relieve that situation, the superintendent of the hospital assigned attendants to sit with her during the day, an unwelcome task for them because Dix was often suspicious and hostile to her caretakers. [23]

When Dix was near death, she begged her doctor, "Don't give me anything. None of those anodynes to dull senses or relieve pain. I want to . . . feel it all. And . . . please tell me when the time is near. I want to know."[24] Dix died on July 17, 1887 at the age of seventy-nine and was buried in Mt. Auburn Cemetery in Cambridge.

In keeping with her wishes, her marble marker gave only her name, Dorothea Lynde Dix. Dr. Charles Nichols wrote "that thus had been laid to rest in the most quiet, unostentatious way the most useful and dedicated woman America had yet produced."[25]

Dix desired to be anonymous in death as she had in life. She treasured her privacy and never sought acclaim, for example, not allowing hospitals to be named after her. On the other hand, she did allow Dixmont Hospital near Pittsburgh (now closed) to be named after her grandfather, and later, Dix Hill Hospital in Raleigh, NC.[26] Nor had Dix posed for busts, and she had resisted having her portrait made. When Sarah Josepha Hale asked Dix for information for her book, *Lives and Character of Distinguished Women*, Dix refused to accommodate her, writing Hale that such an undertaking would cause her pain and serious annoyance, invade her personal rights, and offend her sense of propriety. Dix commented that she prized reputation over distinction and notoriety and she would not exchange it for fame or transient popular applause."[27]

Of her fame, Dix wrote to Anne Heath, "People here seem to think I have done a great work. Perhaps I have. I know it is certainly very satisfying and I feel right about it at heart, and a thousand times happier than if I had wasted my time doing nothing for the good of others.[28] Dix never lost her ability to personally relate to the sufferings of the insane as shown by her writing while in England. "If I am cold, they too are cold, if I am weary, they are distressed, if I am alone, they are abandoned."[29]

END NOTES

i.   3.

ii.   Ibid.

End Notes: Dix

1. Lauren S. Bahr, Editorial Director, (*American National Biography, Oxford University Press, 1999 Oxford*).635.

2. Penny Coleman, *The Crusade of Dorothea Lynde Dix, Crozet, Va.: Shoe Tree Press* (1992):110.

3. Dorothy Clarke Wilson, *Stranger and Traveler, Boston: Little Brown and Company (1975)*:27.

4. Coleman, 16.

5. Ibid., 17.

6. Wilson, 7.

7. Ibid., 17.

8. Ibid., 25.

9. Thomas J. Brown, Dorothea Dix, *New England Reformer* (Cambridge: Harvard University Press): 7.

10. Coleman, 20.

11. Wilson, 38.

12. Ibid, 40.

13. Ibid., 43.

14. Ibid., 84.

15. Wilson, 54.

16. Wayne Viney,Unitarian Univerisalist Historical Society, 1999-2004 *http://www.uua.org/uuhs/duub/articles/dorothea dix.html:2.*

17. John A. Garraty, Editor, (American *National Biography Vol. 6 NY Oxford University Press, NY 1999*) 635. Coleman, 26.

18. Coleman, 26.

19. Viney. 1.Brown, 15.

20. Penny Coleman, 28.

21. Garraty, 15.

22. Wilson, 53.

23. Brown, 13.

24. Ibid., 14.

25. Ibid., 24.

26. Ibid., 25.

27. Ibid., 26.

28. Ibid., 25.

29. Ibid., 125.

30. Wilson., 89.

31. Veney, 1.

32. Brown, 35.

33. Ibid., 38.

34. Brown, 39.

35. Ibid., 40.

36. Ibid., 39.

37. Wilson, 70.

38. Brown, 20.

39. Wilson, 72.

40. Brown, 60.

41. Wilson, 76.

42. Ibid., 84.

43. Ibid.,74.

44. Brown, 66.

45. Ibid., 64.

46. Garraty, 635.

47. Brown, 67.

48. *The American National Biography*, vol.6, (New York, NY: Oxford University Press, Inc.:635.

49. Wilson, 85.

50. Garraty, 635.

51. Wilson, 127.

52. Brown, 93.

53. Garraty, 636.

54. Brown, 88.

55. Wilson, 125.

56. Brown, 96.

57. Ibid., 124.

58. Wilson, 138.

59. Henry M. Hurd, etal., *Institutional Care of the Insane in the United States and Canada,vol.1*,(Baltimore, Md.:the John Hopkins Press,1916.):113.

60. Wilson, 155.

61. Hurd, 112.

62. Wilson, 73.

63. Hurd, 112.

64. Brown, 103.

65. Ibid., 106.

66. Ibid., 107.

67. Ibid., 108.

68. Ibid., 109.

69. Hurd, 112.

70. Coleman, 78.

71. Brown, 148.

72. Brown, 170.

73. Ibid., 178.

74. Ibid.,172.

75. Ibid., 184.

76. Wilson, 186.

77. Brown, 186.

78. Brown, 149.

79. Hurd, 112.

80. Brown, 160.
81. Wilson, 187.
82. Brown, 192.
83. Wilson, 178.

End Notes: Stribling

1. Annual Report of the Board of Directors, Asst. Physician and Steward of the Western Lunatic Asylum of Va.,1873; Western Archives, Staunton, Va.6.

2. Dr. Francis T. Stribling's letter to Dorothea L. Dix, July 23, 1858, Library of Virginia.

3. Annual Report,1848.34.

4. Stribling letter to Dix, March 8, 1853.

5. Dr. Hobart Hansen, Superintendent of Western State Hospital, Received at Western State Library, Dec, 5. 1967: Staunton, Va. Western State.4.

6. Francis Rodgers Huff Griffin, *Wagon Roads to Western Mountains of Va.*, Verona, Va.:McClure Printing Co. (1975) 57.

7. Staunton, *The Vindicator*, July 24,1874.

8. Griffin, 57.

9. Report, 1873-74, 6.

10. Staunton, *The Vindicator*, July, 1874.

11. Augusta County Marriage Records, May 17,1831, Augusta County Courthouse.

12. Stribling Family Bible (Charlottesville, Va.:University of Virginia Special Collections Library, Alderman Library).

13. Report, 1873-74, 7.

14. Report, 1836, 8.

15. Report, 1837, 1.

16. Report, 1841, 5.

17. Report, 1837, 1.

18. Ibid.,4.

19. Report, 1841, 8.

20. Shomer S. Zwelling, *Quest for a Cure: The Public Hospital in Williamsburg, Virginia, 1773-1885*, (Williamsburg, Va.:The Colonial Williamsburg Publishing, 1886):9.

21. Norman Dain, *Disordered Minds, The First Century of Eastern State Hospital in Williamsburg, Va.*, Published by the Colonial Williamsburg Foundation, Charlottesville, Va.:University Press of Virginia, 9.

22. R. Given Fulton's letter to Stribling, December 12, 1844.

23. Dain, 102.

24. V.M. Randolph, U.S.N., *A Candid Inquiry Into Some of the Abuses and Cruelties Now Existing and Practiced in the Staunton, Va, Insane Asylum, Together With a Few Humble Suggestions for their Correction.*(Richmond, Va.: Colin and Nowlan:1852, Charlottesville, Va.:University of Virginia Special Collections Library.) 2-3.

25. President and Court of Directors' Report to the Virginia Legislature, "Investigations of Charges Brought by Captain Randolph Against Western State, January 1853": Staunton, Virginia, Western State Hospital, 39.

26. Stribling's report to his directors, 1869-71, Table 3.

27. Report, 1863-64.

28. Henry M. Hurd, et.al.*Institutional Care of the Insane in the United States and Canada.* Vol.3,(Baltimore, Md.;)726.

29. Joseph Waddell, *Historical Atlas of Augusta County, Virginia-Maps from the Original Survey by Jed Hotchkiss, top Engr. Its Annals by Joseph Waddell-Physiography by Jed Hotchkiss*, C.& M.E. Illustrated. (Chicago, Il.): Waterman, Watkins & Co., 1885., 508.

30. Boston, *Enquirer and Examiner newspaper*, June 23, 1868.

31. *First Session of Forty-first Congress, 1869, Private Acts.* 4 March, AD1869, 10 April 1869, 625.

32. Report of 1869-70 and 1870-71, 8.

33. American Journal of Insanity, 1873-74., 180.

34. Ibid., 3.

35. Staunton, Va., *The Vindicator*, July 24, 1874.

36. *The Southern Churchman*, 1874, 5.

37. Directors, Western State Hospital, 1873-74, 5.

38. Memorial, Alexandria, Va.
39. Staunton, *The Vindicator*, July 24, 1974.
40. Ibid., March 1, 1889.

End Notes: Clarifying Information Among Letters:

1. Stribling to Dix, March 8, 1853.
2. Stribling to Governor Wise, January 7, 1857.
3. Wilson, 209.
4. Ibid., 212.
5. Ibid., 209.
6. Hurd, 120.
7. Mariners' Museum.
8. Garraty, 636.
9. Wilson, 241.
10. Ibid., 246.
11. Brown, 227.
12. Ibid., 241.
13. Wilson, 248.
14. Wilson, 251.
15. Brown, 194.
16. Wilson, 253.
17. Stan Cohen, *Historic Springs of the Virginia's*, (Charleston West Virginia.: Pictorial Histories Publishing Company, 1981) vii.
18. J.J. Moorman's, *Virginia Springs and Springs of the South and West*, J.B. Lippincott, 1859, 72.
19. Ibid., 57.
20. Coleman, 35.
21. Ibid., 103.

End Notes: Dorothea Dix: During and After The Civil War:

1. Coleman, 109.
2. Ibid, 110.

3.   Wilson, 273.

4.   Ibid., 272.

5.   Ibid., 270.

6.   Ibid., 271.

7.   Garraty, 637.

8.   Coleman, 111.

9.   Samuel Bell Waugh, http://www.civilwar.si.edu/leaders_dix.html.,2.

10.   Wilson, 299.

11.   Garraty, 637.

12.   Frank Stribling Letter to Dix, December 17, 1874.

13.   Frank Stribling letter to Dix, January 17, 1865.

14.   Mrs. Henrietta Stribling's letter to her son Frank.

15.   Coleman, 119.

16.   Ibid., 122.

17.   David J. Rothman, *The Discovery of the Asylum:* (Boston-Toronto:Little Brown and Company) 1971: 268.

18.   Ibid., 269.

19.   Ibid., 266.

20.   Wilson, 138.

21.   Ibid., 329.

22.   Ibid., 334.

23.   Ibid., 336.

24.   Ibid., 341.

25.   Ibid., 342.

26.   Coleman, 73.

27.   Wilson, 187.

28.   Ibid., 235.

29.   Ibid., 93.

DIX LETTERS TO STRIBLING

A great deal of information from Western State is now at the Library of Virginia. The Dix-Stribling letters can be accessed as follows: "Records of Western State Hospital, 1825-1996. Accession 31030, State Records Collection, The Library of Virginia, Richmond, Va. 23219."

Prior to moving the Dix letters to the Library of Virginia, Western State Hospital gave the author permission to use the following ones in *Dorothea Dix-Dr. Francis T. Stribling: An Intense Friendship*. The dates of those letters follow.

January 29, 1849
February 7, 1852
April 23, 1852
May 14, 1852
June 24, 1852
July 19, 1852
August 11, 1852
April 11, no date, probably 1853-54 (..Land Hotel..)
April 2, probably 1854
March 9, 1858
May 7, 1858
1858, month unknown (..Rockbridge Alum..)
July 4, 1858
July 6, 1858
1858, probably July (..White Sulphur Springs..)
Undated and incomplete letter
July 15, 1858
April 18, probably 1859
November 22, 1859
December 9, 1859
November 26, 1860

The library of Virginia gave permission to use the following letters.

July 23, 1850
Sept. 21, 1850
"Friday" only date
April 2, probably 1854
"Thursday" only date, probably 1858
January, 1871, note by unknown person
January or February, 1874

The following letters were incomplete.
No date, but "Rockbridge Alum." Most probably 1858
No date, but "White Sulphur Springs. Most probably 1858
No date, "just arrived from Raleigh."

DR. STRIBLING'S LETTERS TO DIX

All of the Stribling letters to Dix are at Houghton Library and are used "By Permission of Houghton Library, Harvard University, Cambridge, MA." The access number for the following letters is: bMS Am 1838 (613) and (613A).

July 19, 1850
August 16, 1852
March 8, 1853
February 1, 1854
July 23, 1858
January 11, 1859
March 12, 1859

The Houghton Library also has the following two letters written by Stribling's son Frank to Dix and a third letter written by Mrs. Henrietta Stribling to her son.

FRANK STRIBLING'S LETTERS TO DIX

December 17, 1864 and January 13, 1865. bMS Am 1838 (613A) and bMS Am 1383 (614) and (613A) for paperbacks.

MRS. HENRIETTA STRIBLING'S LETTER TO SON FRANK

December 1, 1864 bMS Am 1838 (613A) and bMS 1383 (614) and (613A) for paperback.

BIBLIOGRAPHY

American Journal of Insanity, vols. 1844-1874.

Bahr, Lauren S., editorial director, Bernard Johnson, editor-in-chief and Louise H. Bloomfield, executive editor.
The American National Biography, Vol. 6, (New York, N.Y. Oxford University Press, Inc.

Brown, Thomas J. *Dorothea Dix: New England Reformer.*(Cambridge:Harvard University Press.

Bumb, Jean, "Dorothea Dix." *www.webster.edu/~woolfkm.dorotheadix.htgml;4.*

Central Lunatic Asylum. Board of Directors and Medical Supervisor *Annual Report*. 1870-71: Richmond, Va.

Coleman, Penny. *Breaking the Chain: The Crusade of Dorothea Lynde Dix*. Crozet, Va.: Shoe tree Press, imprint of Betterway Publication, Inc.

Congress, *First Session of the Forty-first Congress*, *Private Acts*, 4 March AD1869,10 April 1869.

Dain, Norman. *Disordered Minds: The First Century of Eastern State Hospital in Williamsburg, Va. 1766-1866*. Williamsburg, Va.: Colonial Williamsburg Foundation. Charlottesville, Va.: Distributed by the University Press of Virginia.

Dix, Dorothea. Letters to Stribling, Richmond, Library of Virginia.

Druff, Dr. James H. "Francis Taliaferro Stribling Papers at Western State Hospital." Address delivered at the semi-annual meting of the Augusta Historical Society, May 18, 1966 and *Augusta Historical Bulletins* 1-6. Staunton, Va.: Augusta County Historical Society. vol.2 no.2. 19.

Dunn, Nancy Feys. "The Era of Moral Therapy at Western State Hospital."
    Chicago, MA thesis, De Paul University.

Galt, Dr. John Minson
    "On the Propriety of Admitting the Insane of Two Sexes into the
    Same Lunatic Asylum." *American Journal of Insanity* 7 (1849-50).
    "The Farm at St. Anne." *American Journal of Insanity* 10 (1854-55).

Garraty, John A. Editor, (*American National Biography, Vol 6, NY Oxford
    University Press*, New York 1999.)

Green, E.M., MD. "Psychoses Among Negroes, A Comparative Study,"
    Institutional Care of the Insane, vol.3.

Griffin, Francis Rodgers Huff. *Wagon Roads to Western Mountains of Virginia*.
    Verona, Va.: McClure Printing Co. 1975.

Hansen, Dr. Hobart G. "Article on Stribling." Received at Western State
    Library, Dec. 5, 1967: Staunton, Va.: Western State Hospital.

Hurd, Henry et.al. editors. *The Institutional Care of the Insane in the United
    States and Canada.*Volumes 1-4. Baltimore, Md.: The John Hopkins
    Press. 1916.

Jarvis, Dr. Edward.
    "On the Comparative Liability of Males and Females to Insanity,
    and Their Comparative Curability and Mortality When Insane"
    American Journal of Insanity 7 (1850-51).
    "Insanity Among the Colored Population of the Free States."
    American Journal of Insanity 8 (1851-52).

Lewis J. Johnson, Abstract based on "A Commission of Inquiry and Advice
    in Respect to Sanitary Interests of the United States Forces,"
    Encyclopedia of Women's History and hhtpL/www.netwalk.com/jpr/
    history1.htmpl.

McIlhany, Hugh Milton, Jr. *Some Virginia Families: Being Genealogies of the
    Kinney, Stribling, Trout, McIlhany, Millton, Rogers, Tate, Snickers, Taylor,
    McCormick and other Families of Virginia*. Baltimore: Genealogical
    Publishing Co. 1962.

McIlhenny, J. J. "The Various Means of Restraints." *American Journal of
    Insanity* 16 (1850-51). *Virginia Regimental Histories Series, First
    Edition*. Lynchburg, Va.: H. E. Howard, Inc.

Newspapers, Virginia: (Staunton) *the Vindicator, Staunton Spectator, Valley-Virginian*; (Richmond) *Richmond Inquirer*; (Alexandria) name unknown, *reprinted in Staunton Spectator, Gordonsville Gazette*, reprinted in *Staunton Spectator, Enquirer and Examiner* Boston, MA.

Powell, Louise Papers. University of Virginia Alderman Library Special Collections: Stribling notes (cards) regarding Medical School at the University of PA. Stribling unpublished correspondence regarding his attempt to obtain a political disability, etc. Charlottesville, VA.

Prison Discipline Society of Boston, Managers. *Annual reports*, Boston: T.R. Marvin. 1826-1854.

Captain Randolph, V.M., U.S.N. *A Candid Inquiry into Some of the Abuses and Cruelties Now Existing and Practiced in the Staunton, Virginia Insane Asylum, Together with A Few Humble Suggestions for Their Correction*, Richmond, Va.: Colin and Nowlan, 1852. Copy. University of Virginia Alderman Library Special Collections.

Rothman, David J. *The Discovery of the Asylum: Social Order and Disorder in the New Republic* Boston et.al: Little Brown and Company.

Slave Schedule of Staunton, Virginia. 1860.

Stribling, Francis T.

> *Annual Reports to Western State Board of Directors*, Staunton, Va.: Western State Hospital.
>
> Letters to Dorothea Dix. Houghton Library Harvard University. Cambridge.
>
> "Qualifications and Duties of Attendants of the Insane." *Journal of Insanity* 9 (1852-53).
>
> Speech. *Boston Enquirer & Examiner*. June 23, 1868.

Stribling, Frank. Letters to Dorothea Dix, Houghton Library Harvard University: Cambridge.

Stribling, Henrietta.Letter to son, Frank Stribling. Houghton Library Harvard University. Cambridge.

Stribling Family Bible. Slave births. Mss 779. University of Virginia Special Collections Alderman Library. Charlottesville, VA.

Francis T. Stribling, R.F. Baldwin, Archibald M. Fauntleroy and R. H. Hamilton, *Regulations, Orders, 1854-1883*. Staunton,Va. Western State Hospital.

Virginia Legislature. *Doc. No. 1. Governor's Message and annual reports of the Public Officers of the State and of the Board of directors, Visitors, Superintendents, and other agents of public institutions or interest of Va., printed under the Code of Virginia.* William F. Ritchie, Public Printer. 1850. 3.

Waddell, Joseph. *Historical Atlas of Augusta County, Virginia—Maps from Original Survey by Jed Hotchkiss, Top. Engr. Its Annals by Joseph A. Waddell—Physiography by Jed Hotchkiss, C.& M.E. Illustrated.* Chicago, Ill: Waterman, Watkins &Co. 1885.

Western State Board of Directors. Annual reports, 1836-1874 Depositions and reports relating to Captain Randolph's charges, miscellaneous letters. Staunton, Va., Western State Hospital.

Ibid., "Investigation of Charges Brought by Captain Randolph Against Western State," January 1853. Staunton, Va.

Wilson, Dorothy Clarke. *Stranger and Traveler, the Story of Dorothea Dix, American Reformer.* Boston-Toronto: Little, Brown and Company.

Zwelling, Shormer S. *Quest for a Cure: The Public Hospital in Williamsburg. Virginia, 1773-1885.*Williamsburg: Colonial Williamsburg Publications, 1986.

INDEX

ACKNOWLEDGMENTS

I want to thank the following people who took time from their busy lives to review my book. In Staunton, Virginia, Ruth Arnold, head of the Staunton Library, Frances Coltrane, retired psychiatric nurse and hospital administrator and Joseph Nutt, author and historian. In Waynesboro, Virginia, Dr. Stephen Howlett.

Also, John Beghtol and Mike Poole at Western State Hospital, Marty Klein at Eastern State Hospital, and Mary Anne Bennett, psychiatric nurse at The University of Virginia Hospital. And special thanks to Erwin Bohmfalk, restaurateur and naturalist.

Because images are such an essential part of my book, I want to thank the numerous staff persons at libraries, museums, and other institutions throughout the country for helping me collect them. The names of their institutions follow.

Boston Athenaeum
Colonial Williamsburg Foundation
Fort Monroe Casement Library
Hampden Historical Society
Houghton Library of Harvard
Library of Virginia
Massachusetts Historical Society
Newport News Mariners' Museum

Virginia School for the Deaf and Blind

And Douglas Atkins at the History of Medicine

Hospitals for the Insane in the following states:

New Jersey

North Carolina

Trenton Psychiatric Hospital

West Virginia

Last, but certainly not least, my daughters Judy Smith of Waynesboro and Diane East of Roanoke, Virginia for their immense help and support.

IMAGES

Image 3
Dorothea L. Dix, age twenty-two.
(By permission of the Houghton Library, Harvard University)

Image 4
Anne Heath
Long-time friend of Dorothea Dix.
(Courtesy Massachusetts Historical Society)

Image 5
Dix Bible.
(Courtesy, Trenton Psychiatric Hospital.)

Image 6
New Jersey Hospital for the Insane.
(Courtesy, State of New Jersey.)

Image 7
The Thirteen Founders of the Association
Of Superintendents of American Institutions
For the Insane.
(Courtesy, Western State Hospital.)

MEMBERS OF THE
ASSOCIATION OF MEDICAL SUPERINTENDENTS
OF
AMERICAN INSTITUTIONS FOR THE INSANE.

Image 8
Dorothea Dix Surrounded by Superintendents of Asylums
Additional views listed below in appendices.
(Courtesy, Western State Hospital.)

Image 9
Stribling Springs.
Beyer, Edward, 1820-1865, Album of Virginia.
(Richmond) ca. 1858.
(Courtesy, The Library of Virginia.) call no.F230.857.

Image 10
The University of Virginia.
Howe, Henry, 1816-1893.
Charleston, S.C., W. R. Babcock.
(Courtesy, The Library of Virginia.) call no. F226 H84 1849.

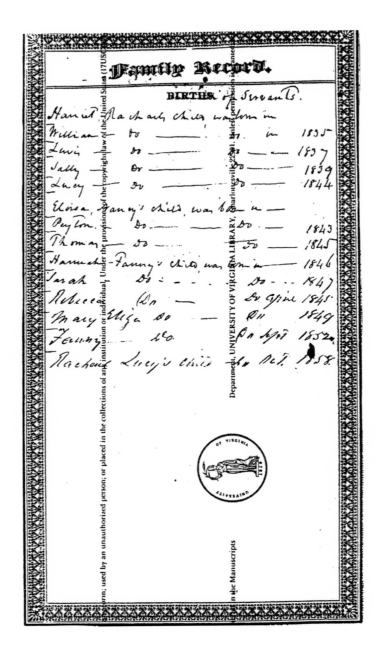

Image 11
Stribling Family Bible.
Female slaves with names and
Birth dates of their children.
(Courtesy, University of Virginia Library.)

Image 12
Western State Hospital, 1838.
Original R.C. Long, prepared by A. C. Smith.
From: Henry Howe, 1816-1893.
(Courtesy, The Library of Virginia.) call no. F226. H84 1849.

Image 13
Western State Hospital, 1849.
(Courtesy, The Library of Virginia.)

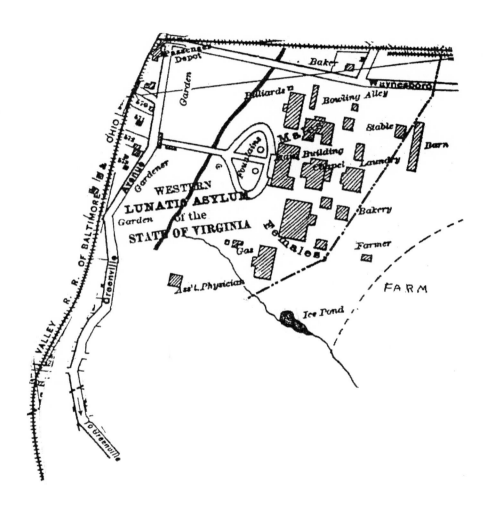

Image 14
Sketch of Western State Hospital Grounds, 1885.
(Courtesy, Western State Hospital.)

Image 15
Western State, Contemporary view of main building.
(Courtesy, Western State Hospital.)

Image 16
Chapel at Western State Hospital.
(Courtesy, Western State Hospital.)

Image 17
Organ still in Chapel at Western State Hospital.
(Courtesy, Western State Hospital.)

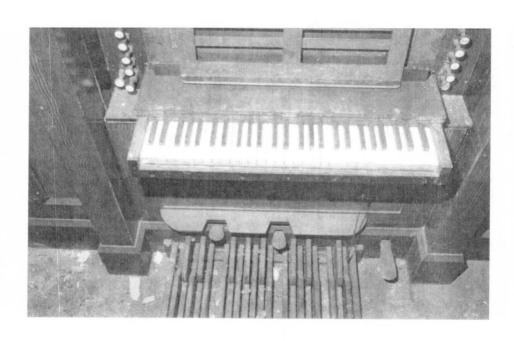

Image 18
View of Organ Showing Damage.
(Courtesy, Western State Hospital.)

Image 19
The Virginia Institution for the Deaf and Blind.
Painted by Charles Wesley Bears.
(Courtesy, The Virginia Institution for the Deaf and the Blind.)

Image 20
Portrait of Dr. John Minson Galt 11.
Painted by Francis Miller White.
(Courtesy of Eastern State Hospital.)

Image 21
Eastern State Hospital, View, 1850's.
(Courtesy, Colonial Williamsburg Foundation.)

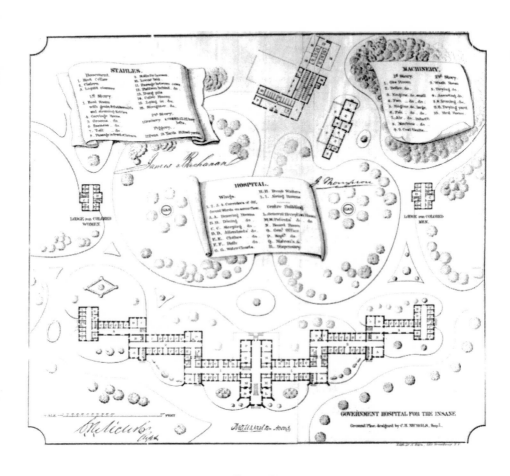

Image 22
Government Hospital for the Insane,
Ground plan designed by C.H. Nichols, 1852.
(Courtesy, St. Elizabeth's Hospital.)

Proposed Front Elevation, 1852

Image 23
Government Hospital for the Insane,
Center Building, Proposed Front Elevation, 1852.
(Courtesy, St. Elizabeth's Hospital.)

Image 24
U.S.M. Steamship "Artic."
(Courtesy of Newport News Mariner's Museum.)

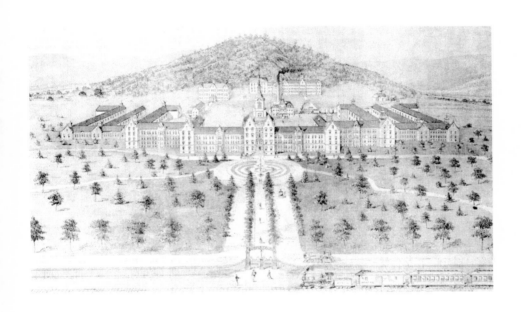

Image 25
West Virginia Hospital for the Insane.
(Courtesy, West Virginia State Archives Collection.)

Image 26
North Carolina Hospital for the Insane.
(Courtesy, The North Carolina State
Archives.) N.75.l. 288.

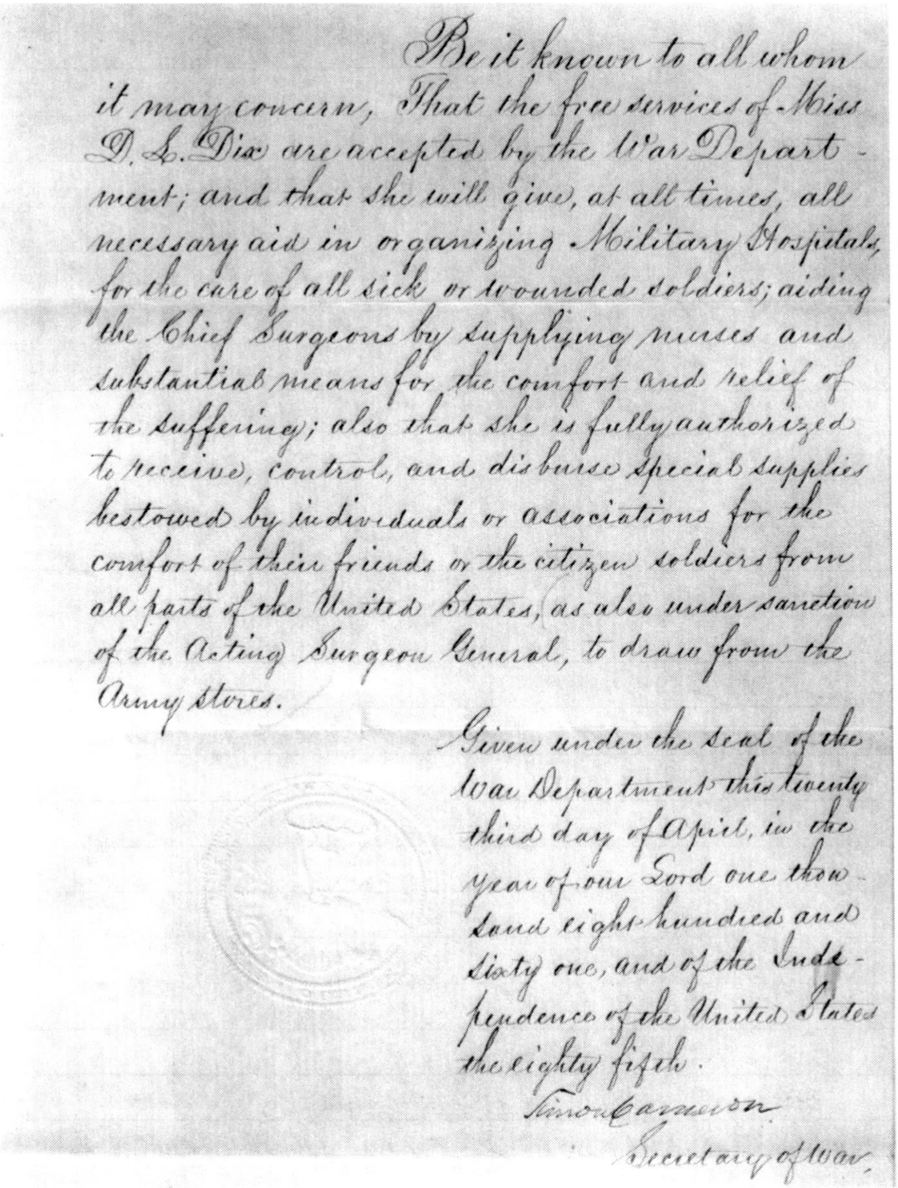

Be it known to all whom it may concern, That the free services of Miss D. L. Dix are accepted by the War Department; and that she will give, at all times, all necessary aid in organizing Military Hospitals, for the care of all sick or wounded soldiers; aiding the Chief Surgeons by supplying nurses and substantial means for the comfort and relief of the suffering; also that she is fully authorized to receive, control, and disburse special supplies bestowed by individuals or associations for the comfort of their friends or the citizen soldiers from all parts of the United States, as also under sanction of the Acting Surgeon General, to draw from the Army stores.

Given under the seal of the War Department this twenty third day of April, in the year of our Lord one thousand eight hundred and sixty one, and of the Independence of the United States the eighty fifth.

Simon Cameron

Secretary of War.

Image 27
Secretary of War Simon Cameron declares Dorothea Dix Head of Union Nurses.
(By Permission of The Houghton Library, Harvard University." bMS Am 1838 (961).

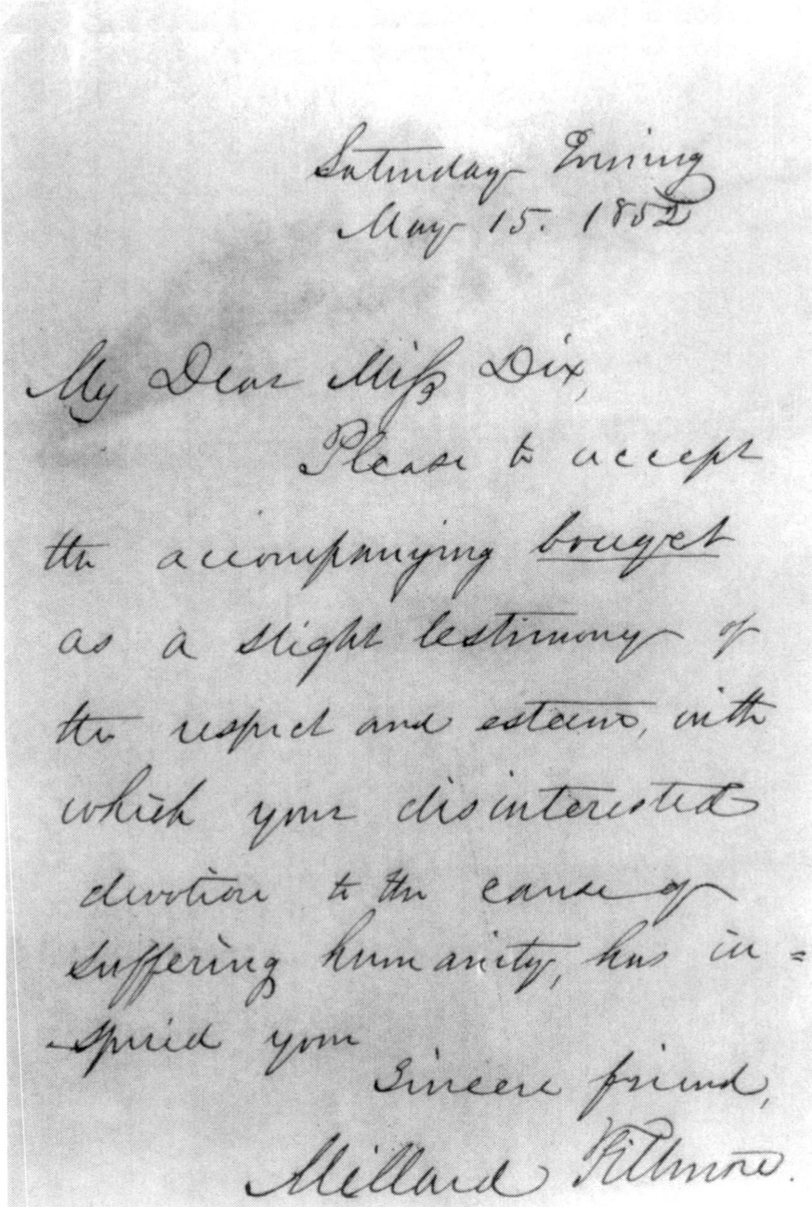

Saturday Evening
May 15. 1852

My Dear Miss Dix,

Please to accept the accompanying bouquet as a slight testimony of the respect and esteem, with which your disinterested devotion to the cause of suffering humanity, has inspired your

Sincere friend,
Millard Fillmore.

Image 28
Note to Dix from President Millard Fillmore dated 15 May 1852.
(By Permission of the Houghton Library.
Harvard University." bMS Am 1838 (228).

Image 29
Painting of Fort Monroe Post Hospital.
15 September, 1862.
(Courtesy, Fort Monroe Casement Museum.)

Image 30
The General Hospital at Fortress Monroe.
Surgeons Dr. Reed Brockway Bontecou (left)
And Dr. John Meck Cuyler.(right).
(Courtesy of Fort Monroe Casement Museum.)

Image 31
Laying the Corner Stone for the Soldiers Monument at
Hampton, Virginia, October 3, 1867.
Sketched by F. Diedmas.
(Courtesy of Fort Monroe Casement Museum.)

Image 32
Monument to the Union War Dead.
Hampton National Cemetery.
(Courtesy of Fort Monroe Casement Museum.)

Image 33
Coach given by Dix to The Illinois Hospital for the Insane.
"By permission of the Houghton Library.
Harvard University." bMS Am 1838 (994).

The Hampden Historical Society

honors

DOROTHEA LYNDE DIX

Humanist, Pioneer, Reformer

BIRTHPLACE OF DOROTHEA L. DIX

BORN HAMPDEN, MAINE
APRIL 4, 1802

FIRST DAY OF ISSUE - SEPT. 23, 1983

Image 34
Birthplace of Dorothea Dix.
(Courtesy, Hampden Historical Society.)

Image 35
Envelope containing stamp issued
September 23, 1983, honoring Dorothea Lynde Dix.
(Courtesy, Hempstead Historical Society.)

APPENDICES

The following images show expanded views of the superintendents shown as a group in Image 8 and also identifies them.

Image 36
Appendix A. Dix and Superintendents, upper-left quadrant.

Image 37
Appendix B. Dix and Superintendents, upper-right quadrant.

Image 38
Appendix C. Dix and Superintendents, lower-left quadrant.

Image 39
Appendix D. Dix and Superintendents, lower-right quadrant.

APPENDIX E

*Identification of superintendents shown as a group
in Image 8 and separately in Image 36-39*

A.

43. Andrews, J. B., Buffalo State Hospital, Buffalo, N. Y., 1880—

5. Archibald, O. Wellington, North Dakota Hospital for the Insane, Jamestown, June 27, 1883—

62. Arnold, John A., King's County Institutions at Flatbush and St. Johnland, N. Y., Feb. 1, 1887.

114. Atwood, Le Grand, St. Louis Insane Asylum, St. Louis, Mo., July 20, 1886—

71. *Awl, Wm. M., Columbus Asylum for the Insane, Columbus, O., 1838–1850.

B.

112. Baker, Lucius W., " Riverview," Baldwinville, Mass.

14. Bancroft, J. P., New Hampshire Asylum for the Insane, Concord, N. H., July 15, 1857—June 1, 1882.

13. Bancroft, C. P., New Hampshire Asylum for the Insane, Concord, N. H., June 1, 1882—

19. Bartlett, Cyrus K., Minnesota Hospital for the Insane, St. Peter, Minn., 1868—

87. *Bell, Luther V., McLean Asylum for the Insane, Somerville, Mass., Dec. 11, 1836—March 16, 1856.

111. Bemis, Merrick, " Herbert Hall," Worcester, Mass.

113. Bishop, B., State Insane Asylum, Reno, Nev., April 1, 1883—

172. *Black, Harvey, South Western Lunatic Asylum, Marion, Va., March 1, 1887—Oct. 19, 1889.

170. Blackford, Benj., Western Lunatic Asylum, Staunton, Va., 1890—

10. Blanchard, Edward S., Insane Hospital, Charlottetown, Prince Edward Island.

80. Blanchard, James A., "Inebriates' Home," Fort Hamilton, N. Y.

60. Blumer, G. Alder, State Lunatic Asylum, Utica, N. Y., Dec. 14, 1886—

6. Booth, Charles E., Northern Hospital for the Insane, Winnebago, Wis., 1887—

73. *Brigham, Amariah, State Lunatic Asylum, Utica, N. Y., Sept. 9, 1842—Sept. 8, 1849.

85. Brooks, H. I., Hospital for the Insane, Elgin, Ill., 1890—

76. *Brown, D. Tilden, Bloomingdale Asylum, New York City, N. Y., 1852–1877.

109. Brown, John P., Taunton Lunatic Hospital, Taunton, Mass., March 1, 1878—

49. *Browne, W. T., State Insane Asylum, Stockton, Cal., Oct. 10, 1883—Feb. 22, 1886.

168. Bryce, P., Alabama Insane Hospital, Tuska-

7. Buckmaster, S. B., Wisconsin State Hospital for the Insane, Mendota, Wis., July, 1864 1890

---

165. Burgess, L. A., Insane Asylum, Jackson, La., 1869–1874.

58. Burgess, T. J. W., Protestant Asylum for the Insane, Montreal, Quebec, May 1, 1890—

38. Burr, C. B., Eastern Michigan Asylum, Pontiac, Mich., 1889—

27. Burrell, D. R., " Brigham Hall," Canandaigua, N. Y., 1876—

105. *Butler, John S., Connecticut Retreat for the Insane, Hartford, Conn., May 13, 1843—Oct. 20, 1873.

139. Buttolph, H. A., State Asylum for the Insane, Morris Plains, N. J., 1876–1885.

C.

150. Callender, John H., Central Hospital for the Insane, Nashville, Tenn., 1870—

154. Camden, T. B., West Virginia Hospital for the Insane, Weston, Va., July 1, 1871—May 16, 1881.

152. Campbell, Michael, Eastern Hospital for the Insane, Knoxville, Tenn.

3. *Carpenter, Horace, Oregon State Insane Asylum, Salem, Or., Oct. 23, 1883—May 1, 1886.

100. Carriel, H. F., Illinois Central Hospital for the Insane, Jacksonville, Ill., July, 1870—

82. *Catlett, Geo. C., State Lunatic Asylum, No. 2, St. Joseph, Mo., 1874–1886.

110. Chandler, Geo., Worcester Lunatic Hospital, Worcester, Mass., July, 1846—April, 1856.

93. Channing, Walter, Private Hospital for Mental Diseases, Brookline, Mass.

155. Chapin, John B., Pennsylvania Hospital for the Insane, Philadelphia, Penn., 1884—

156. Chase, Robert H., State Hospital for the Insane, Norristown, Penn., 1880—

81. Clark, Asa, Pacific Asylum, Stockton, Cal.

56. Clark, Daniel, Asylum for the Insane, Toronto, Ont., Canada, 1875—

117. Clark, John H., Dayton Asylum for the Insane, Dayton, O., March 1, 1874—May, 1876.

40. Clarke, Chas. K., Asylum for the Insane, Kingston, Ont., Canada, 1885—

131. Clarke, F. H., Eastern Kentucky Lunatic Asylum, Lexington, Ky.

47. Cleaveland, Joseph M., Hudson River State Hospital, Poughkeepsie, N. Y., 1867—

115. *Clements, Joshua, Dayton Asylum for the Insane, Dayton, O.

57. Clouston, T. S., Morningside, Edinburgh, Scotland. Honorary member of the Association.

28. *Cook, Geo., " Brigham Hall," Canandaigua, N. Y., 1855–1876.

92. Cowles, Edward, McLean Asylum for the Insane, Somerville, Mass., Dec. 1, 1879—

138. Curwen, John, State Hospital for the Insane, Warren, Penn., July 7, 1881—

90. Cutter, Nehemiah, Pepperell, Mass.

D.

127. Denny, James H., Connecticut Retreat for the Insane, Hartford, Conn., 1872–1874.

84. Dewey, Richard, Illinois Eastern Hospital for the Insane, Kankakee, Ill., 1879—

31. *Dimon, Theodore, State Asylum for Insane Criminals, Auburn, N. Y., Oct. 1, 1879—June 1, 1881.

121. *Dix, Dorothea L., the founder of many institutions for the insane.

161. Dorset, John S., State Lunatic Asylum, Austin, Tex., 1887—

12. Draper, Joseph, Vermont Asylum for the Insane, Brattleboro, Vt., 1873—

E.

88. Earle, Pliny, Northampton Lunatic Hospital, Northampton, Mass., July 2, 1864—Oct. 1, 1885.

67. Eastman, Bernard D., Topeka Insane Asylum, Topeka, Kan., March, 1885—

119. Everts, O., Cincinnati Sanitarium, College Hill, O., 1880—

F.

176. *Fisher, Edw. C., North Carolina Insane Asylum, Raleigh, N. C., 1853–1868.

123. Fisher, Theo. W., Boston Lunatic Hospital, Boston, Mass., Jan. 1, 1881—

63. Fleming, Walter S., King's County Insane Asylum, Flatbush, N. Y., 1889—

G.

103. *Galt, John M., 2d., Eastern Lunatic Asylum, Williamsburg, Va., July, 1841—May 18, 1862.

34. Gause, C. O., Kansas State Insane Asylum, Osawatomie, Kan., July 1, 1866—Nov. 30, 1871.

70. Gilman, H. A., Iowa Hospital for the Insane, Mt. Pleasant, Ia., Feb., 1882—

Gerhard, J. Z., Pennsylvania State Lunatic Hospital, Harrisburg, Penn., 1881—

137. Godding, W. W., Government Hospital for the Insane, Washington, D. C., 1877—

143. *Goldsmith, Wm. B., Butler Hospital for the Insane, Providence, R. I., 1886—March 21, 1888.

142. Gorton, Wm. A., Butler Hospital for the Insane, Providence, R. I., 1888—

59. *Gray, John P., State Lunatic Asylum, Utica, N. Y., July 19, 1854—Nov. 29, 1886.

175. Grissom, Eugene, North Carolina Insane Asylum, Raleigh, N. C., 1868–1889.

136. Gundry, Richard, Maryland Hospital for the Insane, Catonsville, Md., 1878—

H.

140. Harris, H. C., State Asylum for the Insane, Morris Plains, N. J., 1888—

96. Harrison, D. A., "Breezehurst Terrace," Whitestone, L. I., N. Y., 1890—

16. Harlow, H. M., Maine Insane Hospital, Augusta, Me., 1851–1883.

2. *Hawthorne, J. C., Oregon State Insane Asylum, Salem, Or., 1862–1881.

23. Head, Louis R., Wisconsin State Hospital for the Insane, Mendota, Wis., 1890—

135. Hill, Charles G., Mount Hope Retreat, Baltimore, Md.

53. Hill, Gershom H., Iowa Hospital for the Insane, Independence, Ia., 1881—

141. Hinckley, L. S., Essex County Asylum for the Insane, Newark, N. J.

163. Hooper, P. O., State Lunatic Asylum, Little Rock, Ark., 1885—

44. Howard, E. H., Monroe County Insane Asylum, Rochester, N. Y.

146. Hughes, Chas. H., State Lunatic Asylum, No. 1, Fulton, Mo., 1862–1872.

39. Hurd, Henry M., Eastern Michigan Asylum, Pontiac, Mich., 1878–1879.

158. Hutchinson, H. A., Western Pennsylvania Hospital for the Insane, Dixmont, Penn., 1885—

J.

50. Jacobs, L. W., Kansas State Insane Asylum, Osawatomie, Dec. 1, 1872—Oct. 1, 1873.

149. Jones, J. B., Western Hospital for the Insane, Bolivar, Tenn., Aug. 20, 1889—

164. Jones, J. Welch, Insane Asylum, Jackson, La., 1874—Sept. 3, 1888.

151. Jones, Wm. P., Central Hospital for the Insane, Nashville, Tenn., 1862–1870.

K.

20. Kilbourne, Arthur F., Second Minnesota Hospital for the Insane, Rochester, Minn., 1890—

86. *Kilbourne, E. A., Hospital for the Insane, Elgin, Ill., 1871—Feb. 27, 1890.

133. King, C. W., Dayton Asylum for the Insane, Dayton, O., 1890—

104. *Kirkbride, Thos. S., Pennsylvania Hospital for the Insane, Philadelphia, Penn., January, 1841—Dec. 17, 1883.

51. Knapp, A. H., Kansas State Insane Asylum, Osawatomie, Kan., Nov. 1, 1878—

L.

118. *Landfear, L. R., Dayton Asylum for the Insane, Dayton, O., 1876–1878.

8. *Landor, Henry, Asylum for the Insane, London, Ontario, Can., 1868–1877.

4. Lane, Henry, Oregon State Insane Asylum, Salem, Or., July 1, 1887—

41. La Rue, G. A., Quebec Lunatic Asylum, Mastai, Quebec, 1889—

35. Lee, C. P., Kansas State Insane Asylum, Osawatomie, Kan., Nov. 30, 1871—Dec. 1, 1872.

9. Lett, Stephen, The Homewood Retreat, Guelph, Ontario, Can., Dec. 21, 1883—

68. Lewellen, P. W., Iowa Hospital for the Insane, Clarinda, Ia.

153. Lewis, J. S., West Virginia Hospital for the Insane, Weston, W. Va., Nov. 1, 1888—

36. Long, O. R., Asylum for Insane Criminals, Ionia, Mich., June 1, 1885—

46. Lomax, J. D., Marshall Infirmary, Troy, N. Y., Oct. 12, 1863—

78. Lyon, S. B., Bloomingdale Asylum, New York City, N. Y., 1890—

M.

95. Macomber, John L., Branch of King's County Lunatic Asylum, St. Johnland, N. Y., June, 1890—

30. McDonald, Carlos F., State Asylum for Insane Criminals, Auburn, N. Y., June 1, 1881—July 1, 1889.

75. *McDonald, James, Sanford Hall, Flushing, N. Y., May, 1845–1849.

101. McFarland, Andrew, Oak Lawn Retreat, Jacksonville, Ill., 1872—

24. *Metcalf, W. G., Asylum for the Insane, Kingston, Ontario, Can., July, 1879—Aug. 16, 1885.

174. Miller, J. F., Eastern North Carolina Insane Asylum, Goldsboro, N. C., 1866—

116. Miller, S. J. F., Dayton Asylum for the Insane, Dayton, O.,   —1873.

167. Mitchell, Thos. J., Mississippi State Lunatic Asylum, Jackson, Miss., 1878—

171. Moncure, J. D., Eastern Lunatic Asylum, Williamsburg, Va., 1864—

173. Murphy, P. L., Western North Carolina Insane Asylum, N. C., 1882—

N.

77. *Nichols, Chas. H., Bloomingdale Asylum, New York City, N. Y., 1877–1889.

108. Nims, E. B., Northampton Lunatic Hospital, Northampton, Mass., October, 1885—

P.

124. Page, Chas. W., Danvers Lunatic Hospital, Danvers, Mass., 1888—

125. Paine, N. Emmons, Westborough Insane Hospital, Westborough, Mass., May 1, 1886—

37. Palmer, Geo. C., Michigan Asylum for the Insane, Kalamazoo, Mich., 1878—

48. Parsons, Ralph L., Greenmont, near Sing Sing, N. Y.

83. Patterson, R. J., Bellevue Place, Batavia, Ill., 1867—

166. Perkins, Lewis G., Insane Asylum, Jackson, La., September, 1888—

45. Pilgrim, Chas. W., Willard Asylum for the Insane, Willard, N. Y., 1890—

132. Pollock, Calvin, Dayton Asylum for the Insane, Dayton, O., 1888–1890.

169. Powell, Theophilus O., State Lunatic Asylum, Asylum P. O., Ga., 1879—

107. *Prince, Wm. H., Northampton Lunatic Hospital, Northampton, Mass., Oct. 1, 1857—April 1. 1864.

R.

69. *Ranney, Mark, Iowa Hospital for the Insane, Mt. Pleasant, Ia., 1875–1882.

106. *Ray, Isaac, Butler Hospital for the Insane, Providence, R. I., December, 1846—January, 1867.

159. *Reed, J. A., Western Pennsylvania Hospital for the Insane, Dixmont, Penn., 1857–1884.

17. Reid, Robert K., State Insane Asylum, Stockton, Cal., 1851—Oct. 1, 1856.

52. Reynolds, Albert, Iowa Hospital for the Insane, Independence, Ia., 1872–1881.

134. Richardson, A. B., Athens Asylum for the Insane, Athens, O., 1881–1890.

147. Rodman, James W., Western Kentucky Lunatic Asylum, Hopkinsville, Ky., 1863–1889.

54. Rogers, Joseph G., Northern Indiana Hospital for the Insane, Longcliff, Logansport, Ind.

25. *Roy, F. E., Quebec Lunatic Asylum, Mastai, Quebec, —1889.

65. Rucker, Hiram N., State Insane Asylum, Stockton, Cal., Nov. 1, 1888—

S.

15. Sanborn, Bigelow T., Maine Insane Hospital, Augusta, Me., May, 1883—

144. *Sawyer, John W., Butler Hospital for the Insane, Providence, R. I., 1866—December, 1885.

18. *Shantz, Samuel E., Minnesota Hospital for the Insane, St. Peter, Minn., 1866–1868.

160. Schultz, S. S., State Hospital for the Insane, Danville, Penn., 1868—

64. Shaw, John C., King's County Lunatic Asylum, Flatbush, N. Y., 1879–1887.

33. Shurtleff, G. A., State Insane Asylum, Stockton, Cal., Aug. 5, 1865—Oct. 10, 1883.

128. Smith, Edwin E., Kensett on the Sound, Rowayton, Conn.

126. Stearns, H. P., Connecticut Retreat for the Insane, Hartford, Conn., 1874—

89. *Stedman, Chas. H., Boston Lunatic Hospital, Boston, Mass., Oct., 1842—June, 1851.

94. Stedman, H. R., "Woodbourne," Roslindale, Mass.

42. Steeves, James T., Provincial Lunatic Asylum, St. John, N. B., 1875—

11. Stiles, Henry R., "Hill View," New York.

130. *Stevens, Chas. W., St. Louis Insane Asylum, St. Louis, Mo., Nov. 1, 1883—July 20, 1886.

148. Stone, Bart. a W., Western Kentucky Lunatic Asylum, Hopkinsville, Ky., 1889—

79. Strew, Wm. W., New York City Asylum for the Insane, Blackwell's Island, N. Y., 1877—

120. *Stribling, Francis T., Western Lunatic Asylum, Staunton, Va., 1836–1874.

T.

61. Talcott, Seldon H., State Homœopathic Asylum for the Insane, Middletown, N. Y., 1877—

66. Tenney, A. P., Topeka Insane Asylum, Topeka, Kan., July 1, 1883—March, 1885.

129. Thombs, B. R., State Asylum for the Insane, Pueblo, Col., April 30, 1879—

102. Tobey, H. A., Toledo Asylum for the Insane, Toledo, O., 1884—

91. *Tyler, John E., McLean Asylum for the Insane, Somerville, Mass., Feb. 12, 1858—Feb. 17, 1871.

W.

26. *Waddell, John, Provincial Lunatic Asylum, St. John, N. B., 1849–1875.

122. *Walker, Clement, Boston Lunatic Hospital, Boston, Mass., July 1, 1851—Dec. 30, 1881.

162. Wallace, D. R., North Texas Hospital for the Insane, Terrell, Tex., 1879—

99. Wardner, Horace, Illinois Southern Hospital for the Insane, Anna, Ill., Aug. 6, 1878—Jan. 22, 1890.

1. Waughop, John W., Hospital for the Insane, Fort Steilacoom, Washington, Nov. 1, 1880—

72. *White, Samuel, Hudson, N. Y.

22. Wigginton, R. M., Northern Hospital for the Insane, Winnebago, Wis., 1884–1887.

32. *Wilkie, J. W., State Asylum for Insane Criminals, Auburn, N. Y., Feb. 17, 1870—March 13, 1876.

97. Wilkins, E. T., Napa State Asylum for the Insane, Napa, Cal., March, 1876—

21. Williamson, Alonzo P., Third Minnesota Hospital for the Insane, Fergus Falls, Minn., May 1, 1890—

29. Wise, P. M., St. Lawrence State Hospital, Ogdensburg, N. Y., 1889—

74. *Woodward, Samuel B., Worcester Lunatic Hospital, Worcester, Mass., Oct., 1832—June, 1846.

8. Woodson, C. R., State Lunatic Asylum, No. 2, St. Joseph, Mo., 1890—

55. Wright, C. E., Central Indiana Hospital for the Insane, Indianapolis, Ind.

Y.

145. Young, R. E., State Lunatic Asylum, No. 3, Nevada, Mo.

Note: The historic picture of Dix and the Superintendents shown in Image 8 is located at Western State Hospital. So far, I have been unable to identify the origin or the publisher of this picture. If anyone knows, please advise me at awhisbuf@comcast.net.

The photograph of Image 8 and the enlargements of it shown in the appendices were created by Erwin Bohmfalk of Waynesboro. Erwin has agreed to make them available to others who may desire copies.

His phone number is 540.942.9463 and fax number 540.943.3668.

CPSIA information can be obtained
at www.ICGtesting.com
Printed in the USA
LVOW08s0328251016
510162LV00001B/25/P